THE
RAWVOLUTION
CONTINUES

Also by Matt Amsden

RAWvolution: Gourmet Living Cuisine

ATRIA BOOKS

New York London Toronto Sydney New Delhi

THE RAWVOLUTION CONTINUES

The Living Foods Movement in 150 Natural and Delicious Recipes

Matt and Janabai Amsden

ATRIA BOOKS

Atria Books
A Division of Simon & Schuster, Inc.
1230 Avenue of the Americas
New York, NY 10020

First Atria Books hardcover edition July 2013

ATRIA BOOKS and colophon are trademarks of Simon & Schuster, Inc.

For information about special discounts for bulk purchases, please contact Simon & Schuster Special Sales at 1-866-506-1949 or business@simonandschuster.com.

The Simon & Schuster Speakers Bureau can bring authors to your live event. For more information or to book an event, contact the Simon & Schuster Speakers Bureau at 1-866-248-3049 or visit our website at www.simonspeakers.com.

Designed by Jason Snyder

Manufactured in China

10 9 8 7 6 5 4 3 2 1

Library of Congress Cataloging-in-Publication Data

Amsden, Matt.
    The RAWvolution continues : the living foods movement in 150 natural and delicious recipes / Matt and Janabai Amsden. — First Atria Books hardcover edition.
        pages   cm
    Includes bibliographical references and index.
    1. Cooking (Natural foods)   2. Raw foods.   I. Amsden, Janabai.   II. Title.
    TX741.A5729   2013
    641.6—dc23   2012044513

ISBN 978-1-4516-8700-2
ISBN 978-1-4516-8702-6 (ebook)

We've often referred to our café, Euphoria Loves RAWvolution, as "our love letter to the world" because we hope to inspire others to join us in the delightful, fulfilling, and life-changing passion we call "raw food." We built the café to be a food temple where we could all enjoy healthy food, learn from one another, and build community. We dedicate this book to that community: to all the souls who felt the call and answered and to those who continue to be called to join us in defining a new paradigm of health, joy, and freedom. We could not have had so much fun, magic, and transformation without your participation. We all did this together and what we have co-created will not be forgotten. Thank you for joining us on this journey!

Contents

Introduction

Our Story, or, What the Heck Does
"Euphoria Loves RAWvolution" Mean Anyway? 2

What Are Raw Foods? 7

What's So Great About Raw Foods? 9

Our Philosophy 13

How to Use This Book 17

Stocking Your Raw Kitchen 19

Recipes

Fundamental Recipes 24

Breakfasts, Shakes, & Smoothies 33

Drinks & Elixirs 69

Soups 97

Appetizers 115

Salads & Side Dishes 137

Entrées 163

Kids' Faves 209

Desserts & Sweets 223

Life

Sample Menus 256

On the Road Again (Again):
Traveling and Eating Raw 258

What's Next? Our Hopes for the Future 262

ACKNOWLEDGMENTS 267

GLOSSARY 268

INDEX 272

Introduction

THE REVOLUTION WILL NOT BE MICROWAVED!

Clean Green Super Food
$4.99 a scoop

Chocolate Superfood
$4.99 a scoop

Our Story, or, What the Heck Does "Euphoria Loves RAWvolution" Mean Anyway?

Eutroph (ū' trof), n. One well versed in the science and art of preparing and combining unfired foods; one able to prepare and combine unfired food so as to present it in the daintiest and most aesthetic form without reducing the health-perpetuating and curative properties; one whose profession is to prepare food for the table of the aesthetic unfired-fooder; an unfired food expert.

Eutrophe on (ū-trŏf' on), n. An unfired fooder's eating house; a house where only dainty and aesthetic unfired food is served; an apyrtropher eating-shop.

—terms coined by George Julius Drews, 1912

In the spring of 1998, at the age of 21, Matt was turned on to the concept of raw foods by way of a radio interview with David Wolfe that he heard on the *Howard Stern Show*. He hadn't been ill, nor had he been searching for an alternative to the meat and potatoes, fast-food lifestyle he'd always lived. Still, the logic behind eating raw foods that Wolfe presented resonated with Matt like nothing he'd ever heard. After a few short weeks of research and reading all he could on the subject, Matt committed to a diet of exclusively uncooked plant foods. As inspired as he was, that first year was tough. Enduring cooked food withdrawals during a Canadian winter without an ounce of organic produce or a single other raw fooder within 200 miles was challenging.

top left: George Malkmus and Matt in Toronto, 1999.

left: David Wolfe, Matt, and friends Anahata and Libby in Hawaii, circa 2003.

Kemell

Lexy

Alexis
Thank you so much for being patient with us and helping us choose some wonderful raw food!! We really enjoyed everything we got. My favorite was the dognwrap you recommended and the cookie dough ball. The hummus was fantastic, too! Ken's favorite was the pie, and Lexy's was her strawberry drink! Ok, I guess we loved it all!

P.S. I left my jacket there...

In the r
Lori, Kemell and L

left:
These sweet customers from Ohio created this card and sent it to us after their first visit!

below: An original poem from an ELR customer!

"RAWESOME"
Food reflective of harmony & peace
Without the blood, death, fat, or grease
From yogi tea to Rosemary Twists
Jack only wishes he had food like this
I tasted it once & it made me go vegan.
So stop by Euphoria & let the Rawvolution begin!

Original Work By
Brett W. Pearce

Dedicated to all the wonderful people at EUR !!! RAWk on !!!

Meanwhile, in New York City, Janabai was naturally gravitating to a diet of raw foods herself, after having been diagnosed with irritable bowel syndrome. A vegetarian since age 12, she now found even cooked vegan foods were making her feel ill and only uncooked plant foods made her feel good. As time went by, she studied yoga intensively and fed her produce habit by shopping at the Park Slope Food Coop in Brooklyn. Within a few months, her IBS was gone, never to return.

Canadian winters were beginning to feel incongruous with Matt's ideal of a life lived in the sunshine with access to an abundance of fresh, organic foods. In the summer of 2000, he purchased a one-way ticket to Los Angeles and packed whatever he could fit into a suitcase. He'd never been to L.A., nor did he know anyone there, but he knew that if he was ever going to be involved in the raw food movement, it was going to happen there. And so he headed west.

Janabai too was feeling the urge to move. She, however, headed East, traveling to India in 2001 to delve deeper into her yoga practice and studies. From India, it was on to Southeast Asia. She traveled in Cambodia and Malaysia before accepting a position at a healing retreat center in Koh Phangan, Thailand. For nearly two years, as a resident cleansing counselor and yoga instructor, Janabai helped guests cleanse and detox using raw vegetable juices, and taught classes on smoothies, sprouting, and fermented foods.

In Los Angeles, Matt found the sunshine, mild climate, and abundance of fresh foods he was looking for. The raw food scene he found was alive, but small, and in need of an infusion of new energy. Pioneering raw chef Juliano Brotman had also just moved to Los Angeles and Matt took the opportunity to learn from him. At that point, Matt's experience in the kitchen included flipping burgers and shoveling fries at McDonald's, where he'd worked for a time while in high school. Beyond that, he knew how to cook two things: omelets and French toast. Matt seemed to have a knack for raw food preparation, however, and he soon began creating his own arsenal of raw food recipes and served them to the public at weekly dinner events at Don Kidson's Living Light House in Santa Monica. In time, Matt was also teaching popular raw food preparation classes and prepared the meals at several of David Wolfe's raw food retreats in Hawaii and abroad. Less than a year after arriving in Los Angeles, Matt started his company, RAWvolution, the world's first raw food delivery service. RAWvolution began shipping The Box, prepared raw meals, throughout Los Angeles, but soon expanded to serve the entire United States.

In the winter of 2004, Janabai returned to the United States from her overseas travels and landed in Arizona. She signed on for a three-month stint as resident chef at Gabriel Cousens's Tree of Life Rejuvenation Center. Janabai was in charge of serving three raw meals a day, seven days a week, to each of the 30-plus guests. She also instructed the Tree of Life's live food, chef-certification program, where she taught

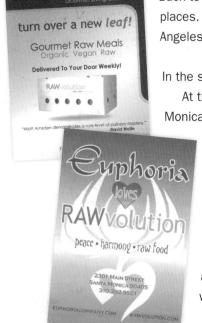

many to create healthful, live cuisine. Once her time at the Tree had concluded, Janabai set herself to deciding where she would go next. Back to New York? Perhaps it was time to continue exploring new places. A friend Janabai had met in India offered a place to stay in Los Angeles. L.A. it was!

In the summer of 2004, Janabai and Matt's paths finally crossed.

At that time, Matt was renting a portion of the kitchen in a Santa Monica restaurant where he served his weekly raw meals and prepared food for the The Box delivery service. Janabai, looking to lend her considerable talents as a raw chef, and having just learned of Matt's business, phoned RAWvolution and asked Matt for a job. Matt informed her that there were no positions available but that she was welcome to volunteer if she liked. This was not the answer she had expected or was hoping for, to say the least. She endured his initial aloofness and agreed that she would volunteer beginning the following week.

Janabai made her way to the restaurant on the agreed-upon day and was directed to the kitchen where Matt was working. As with many conversations between hippies, "what's your sign?" was soon asked. As it turned out, they were both Dragons according to the Chinese zodiac, meaning that they were born in the same year.

"What month?"

"September."

"Me too."

"What day?"

"The 17th."

"Me too!"

They determined that Janabai was about 8½ hours older than Matt. He'd always liked older women so that suited him fine. They soon saw that they had much else in common and, to make a long story at least somewhat shorter, their life of working together began at that moment.

In the ensuing months, Janabai and Matt fell deeply in love and made a home together in Santa Monica.

In 2005, Janabai opened a small retail boutique in Santa Monica that sold packaged raw food snacks, superfoods, herbs, natural body care, and lifestyle products. Called The Euphoria Company, it was wildly successful and soon outgrew the tiny space it occupied.

Janabai and Matt, now engaged to be married, had a few high-class problems. Janabai needed a bigger space for her retail store. Matt needed full-time access to a kitchen for the expanding RAWvolution

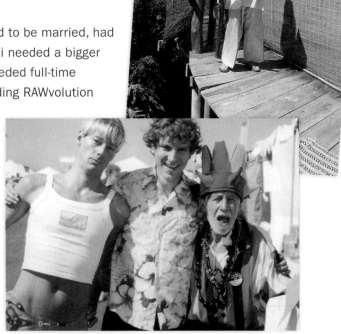

top right: Janabai in Thailand, 2003. Note the copy of Gabriel Cousens' *Conscious Eating* in her hand.

right: Juliano, Matt, and Gypsy Boots in San Diego, 2001.

Raw wedding cake
by Chef Ito of Au Lac,
Fountain Valley, California.

delivery service and people wanted to get their raw food every day, not just once a week when The Box was delivered.

Janabai and Matt soon recognized that a combined effort would prove stronger than the sum of its parts. Thus, Euphoria Loves RAWvolution, Janabai and Matt's love child, was born. Appropriately, Euphoria Loves RAWvolution came into the world on Valentine's Day, 2006. Coincidentally (more likely, it was fate), the building they found to house their new restaurant was the very same one in which they'd met two years before! Maybe that's why people, to this day, say they can "taste the love" in the food that comes out of that kitchen!

Janabai and Matt married on April 8, 2006, less than two months after the opening of ELR. Three months later, Matt's first collection of recipes, *RAWvolution: Gourmet Living Cuisine*, was published.

Since that time, Euphoria Loves RAWvolution has become a pillar in the health-conscious community, serving hundreds of thousands of guests, and has earned local and national recognition for its inventive offerings and environmental awareness. Janabai and Matt still serve as the executive chefs. Along the way, Janabai and Matt have been joined by many kind, hard-working souls who have helped in their way to make Euphoria Loves RAWvolution an ever-expanding tapestry.

In August 2011, a second love child was born. This time, it was simply called RAWvolution. If you're ever in New York City's East Village, please stop in!

Janabai and Matt now live in Topanga Canyon, in the mountains of Los Angeles, with their beautiful twin sons, Cochise and Guthrie, and their beautiful twin poodles Lulu and Sidd.

Much has happened in this 15-year journey living a raw foods lifestyle. Thanks for taking the time to read about some of the best parts of it.

What Are Raw Foods?

Eu'troph-y (ū'trof-y), n. Healthy nutrition; the science which treats of the methods of preparing wholesome food for the moral unfired menu in a dainty and aesthetic form without reducing the health-perpetuating and curative properties; the preparation of the moral, unfired diet.

—term coined by George Julius Drews, 1912

Raw foods, strictly speaking, are any that have not been heated beyond a certain temperature. Different teachers site varying temperatures as the cut-off point. We use 105°F (40°C), though temperatures as high as 118°F have been deemed by other teachers to be considered uncooked and still intact where enzymes, minerals, and vitamins are concerned.

How and why would raw foods get heated past 100°F anyway?

In raw food cuisine, we often use a food dehydrator, which is essentially a low-temperature oven, to gently remove the water from a food while maintaining the food's nutritional and enzymatic properties.

Why remove the water—isn't the water content part of what makes raw foods so healthful?

Water is great. Dehydration is used, not so much to avoid water, but to create dryer, heartier textures. These textures create a contrast to the cool, juiciness of fresh fruits and vegetables and are more filling for those with large appetites, or who are new to raw foods. Dehydrated foods also allow for more creativity and options in the kitchen and add a whole world of variety to one's diet. Dehydrated foods also provide a large measure of convenience as they can be stored, and will remain fresh, for several weeks or longer, reducing the feeling that every raw food meal must begin with an enormous amount of prep.

In order to be considered raw, a food must only be uncooked. This means raw animal foods would qualify—right?

They would. However, we promote a vegetarian and vegan diet, and the recipes in this book contain no animal-derived ingredients.

Does raw food include food grown in any manner?

Yes, although we strongly prefer (really demand) organics in our own lives. We also love food that has been grown biodynamically and on local, family farms. In creating the recipes in this book, you'll use whatever you have access to, but we urge you to choose organics and family-farmed produce whenever possible.

What about freezing?

Freezing, it seems, does not affect food enzymes the way that cooking does, and like dehydration, allows for contrast of flavor and texture, creativity in the kitchen, and more variety. This does not mean that all raw foods, in their original or prepared states, will retain their palatability when frozen and thawed. The recipes in this collection that advise or require freezing still taste great, if not better, after coming out of the freezer.

What about beer, wine, and other alcoholic beverages? Are they raw?

Beer is not considered raw, as it is brewed. The same goes for hard liquors, as they are distilled. Wine and champagne are considered raw, as they are only fermented and are undistilled. Are they healthful? Should you drink them? That's for you to decide!

Some raw food restaurants serve wines that have been specially paired with their menu items, while many raw health educators suggest that it's better to avoid alcohol of any kind, whether raw or not.

What's So Great About Raw Foods?

Apyrtrophism (ă-pēr′ tro-fizm), n. The practice of living exclusively on an unfired diet for the purpose of maintaining or acquiring health and efficiency; the doctrine of internal or intestinal cleanliness for mental, physical, and moral efficiency.
—term coined by George Julius Drews, 1912

What would be the purpose of a book that provided you with over 150 raw food recipes if it did not attempt to explain why you might want to eat raw foods in the first place?

The most commonly cited benefits of raw foods are the higher levels of nutrients, enzymes, water, antioxidants, and life force they provide, and the creation of a more balanced pH in the body when eaten. These assertions have always resonated with us. There are now hundreds of books and articles that explain these claims in detail. In no short supply, too, are texts that dispute each of these pronouncements.

We, of course, are not biologists, chemists, or nutritionists, so we will not attempt to contribute to the conversation by regurgitating scientific or pseudo-scientific data that we've read elsewhere. We do hope, however, that the scientific findings on raw foods by Edward Howell, Jameth Sheridan, Gabriel Cousens, Karl Eimer, and others, find their way into greater awareness.

What we feel we can competently share with you are our experiences and observations from nearly 30 years of combined experimentation with living foods. Since no two experiences are precisely the same, we present our accounts individually.

Matt

As we mentioned in Our Story (page 2), my raw food journey began in the late 1990s. On July 14, 1998, I began to eat uncooked plant foods *exclusively.* I wanted to eat 100 percent raw foods so I could tell if they were truly working or not. The smallest amount of cooked or processed foods would skew my experiment. The first couple of months were challenging. I will admit that, initially, I felt worse than I had when I was eating fast food and drinking soda every day. I attribute the extreme lethargy I felt to having made such an abrupt transition. However, by the time autumn arrived, and in the years to follow, I felt not only better, I felt like a superhero! I had boundless energy, my complexion became clearer, my hair and nails looked healthier, I never experienced headaches, I rarely caught colds, my sense of smell and taste improved, I became physically stronger, and even the whites of my eyes became whiter!

There were other changes too. My mind had never been clearer. I felt as if a fog had been lifted and that my IQ might have increased by a small amount. I wish I had tested it before and after to see if there was indeed a difference. After all, I can use all the help I can get. I felt like I had found the diet everyone was looking for. I could eat as much as I liked without gaining weight or feeling sluggish, I could eat chocolate for breakfast and feel all the better for it, and I was truly enjoying the raw foods I ate. People would ask me if I missed old familiar favorites from when I ate "normal food." I did not. When what you eat makes you feel great, there's no desire to go back from whence you came. I looked back and realized that I'd gone from eating very poorly and feeling very mediocre, to eating fresh, vibrant, living foods, and feeling great. Feeling great had become my norm and I could barely remember what I had felt like in my former life. Friends would sometimes ask, "If you ate a piece of bread right now, would you, like, die?" I didn't imagine it would be that dramatic but I was curious as to how my body would react and how cooked foods would taste to me. It was time to bring the experiment full circle. Well, not *full* circle. I wasn't about to reintroduce the fast foods, sodas, and sweets I'd enjoyed in my youth, and I wasn't interested in partaking in animal foods. But beginning in the summer of 2010, I started experimenting with cooked vegan foods. I was surprised by my initial reaction. They tasted just okay. I guess I was expecting more. For so many years I watched people react with shock and disbelief when they learned that I did not eat meat, bread, rice, or any of the foods they were certain they could *never* live without. They were equally shocked when they tried raw food dishes that I had made and found that they were "actually pretty good." Though I'd been happy with the foods I was eating, people's reverence for cooked foods had infected my subconscious and I was under the impression that cooked foods were extraordinarily tasty, enjoyable, satisfying, and unmatched in flavor. To me, they tasted just okay. I certainly didn't see what all the fuss was about.

The real surprise came the mornings after I had eaten cooked foods. I would wake up and immediately notice that I felt incredibly sluggish. I felt like something was holding me in bed and my head felt groggy. It would take me a minute or so to realize that it was what I had eaten the day before that was causing this hungover feeling.

Many people are of the impression when they go on a raw food diet that they are becoming something wonderful, or that they are making a great sacrifice for mankind. So I would like to address myself to such people who might be contemplating or who have started a raw food diet. You are not dieting, you are not starving, you are not being a martyr, and you are not even being noble. . . . But for the first time in your life you are showing good common sense about maintaining your health and you are at long last eating proper natural, wholesome, health-giving food.

—John H. Tobe, 1969

That was very telling. I would also notice that my body odor became unpleasant after a few cooked food forays.

I learned a lot through my experimentation and, of course, I'm continually experimenting, learning, and fine-tuning my diet and lifestyle as I and my circumstances change. While I'm fairly certain that a cooked meal here and there won't prove to be my undoing, I am, for the most part, ready to stick to the raw foods that had worked so well for me. My life requires a superhero's energy so I need a superhero's diet!

Janabai

As we mentioned in Our Story (page 2), raw foods helped me reverse a debilitating stomach disorder. I should mention that during the time I was sick, I was eating a completely vegan diet, but with a heavy emphasis on soy, rice, processed vegetables, and wheat products. In fact, I had been a vegetarian and on-again, off-again vegan since age 12. I had always looked at my diet through the perspective of animal rights, though. I was very strongly against eating animals, but I was not very savvy about nutrition. I was living on pasta, soy milk, and veggie burgers. After I switched to a 100 percent raw diet, not only were my stomach problems healed, but every aspect of my health also improved. I began to put on lean muscle for the first time in my life, my skin and hair looked amazing, I became more flexible (which was great for my yoga practice), and I had energy to spare.

Beyond that, I noticed emotional and spiritual changes transforming my life. I felt in tune with the natural world around me in a way I have never imagined possible. My mind calmed and I was able to meditate. I had more patience and compassion for the people around me and also toward myself. I felt inspired to make a difference on a daily basis. I truly feel that the very nature of raw foods enabled my system to function optimally and, because of that, upgrade, there was less stress on my nervous system, which allowed my soul to be heard more clearly than it ever had in my adult life.

In the 12 years since my initial

dive into raw foods, I have been submerged into a world of decadent gourmet foodism, rare fruits, and superfoods; life-changing therapies; and wonderful, unforgettable people. The raw food path has always been there for me, and although I am relaxed about my eating habits and try to eat what is right in each moment, the allure of raw food's superiority and simplicity keeps me on the path. The latest chapter of my life has included my pregnancy, the birth of our twin baby boys, and their subsequent nursing (a full-time job in itself!). During this time, as it is with many expecting mothers, my diet shifted away from many of my favorite foods (generally seaweed, greens, and avocado), and I found myself craving foods I didn't eat as often, like berries and frozen sorbets, kimchi, and coconut yogurt. I also incorporated a lot of extra fats into my diet, including cold-pressed coconut oil with every meal. All along the way, I felt like I was giving my babies the cleanest food possible.

What raw food has brought to my life at its essence is a sense of euphoria. Euphoria is defined as a feeling of happiness specifically experienced through the physical body. This is actually why I chose to use the word "euphoria" in the name of our restaurant. Because yes, I really want a RAWvolution, but it is because raw food has taught me the meaning of euphoria.

We realize that folks get nervous when they feel they are being pushed into a radical lifestyle change that they aren't ready for, being drawn into some kind of food cult, or being denied their favorite foods. However, you must forgive those who would attempt to convert you to the world of the "crudivores." Those of us who have discovered the benefits of raw foods are incredibly excited by the positive changes they've brought to our lives. Imagine finishing the most fantastic book you've ever read and not telling your closest friends about it. It's nearly impossible! Still, you need not worry. We're not here to take away your coffee. What we're really talking about is simply eating more fruits and vegetables. This is not an outrageous idea. Any doctor or nutritionist (not to mention your mother), would advise you similarly. One hundred percent adherence to the exclusion of all other foods is not required! We won't tear up your membership card if you're discovered eating steamed broccoli! We do believe, however, that if you're going to be eating vegetables, you might as well get the most that you can from them by eating them in their whole, raw state. To do otherwise is like running the vacuum over the carpet without turning it on. You're doing all of the work but not getting the full benefit.

Our Philosophy

Apyrtrophy (ă-pēr′ tro-fy), n. The science, art, and practice of living upon unfired fruits, herbs, roots, nuts, and cereals (man's natural food), for perpetuating health, for clearness and saneness of mind; also for the prevention and cure of disease; proved to be the only moral system of diet; the science that teaches how to prepare man's primitive foods in elegant style to suit the tastes of cultured man without reducing their health-perpetuating properties.

—term coined by George Julius Drews, 1912

Health

Raw food is our birthright as Earthlings! Cooking came relatively late in man's history. Most of our evolutionary predecessors and ancestors ate raw food exclusively. In fact, every being on this planet has eaten raw food historically and all but humans and animals in captivity still do so exclusively. Raw food is packed with the highest quality nutrition available. Food in its unadulterated form is perfect, beautiful, and life-giving.

Can you be a raw foodist and be unhealthy? Yes! Of course you can make raw food choices that are unbalanced. Usually those imbalances appear when one limits the diversity of the foods they eat. Like our pre-agrarian, hunter-gatherer ancestors, we do best when we gather different foods daily depending on season and location.

Eating primarily nuts, raw chocolate, fruit, or even avocados can lead to imbalances in the long term. A healthy raw diet depends on diversity. We need to eat a broad spectrum of fruits, vegetables, nuts and seeds, greens, sprouts, seaweeds, superfoods, herbs, and quality oils. Eating seasonally is also important

to a healthy raw diet. If you live in a very cold climate then perhaps winter is not the best time for a tropical fruit feast. Focusing on foods that are grown locally can help to guide you towards making seasonally appropriate choices.

Traditional medical models like Ayurveda and Chinese medicine emphasize a customized approach to healthful eating. Though the focus is often on cooked foods, the general framework of these approaches has a strong resonance with us as they acknowledge the differences in individuals—that every one of us has our own specific body type, body chemistry, and bodily needs.

What may be healthiest for you may not always be 100 percent raw if acquiring it is causing you stress. If you truly cannot find any living food to eat when you're hungry, starving yourself is not the answer. Be willing to adapt your choices to your circumstances, but also remember that our circumstances are often more under our control than we sometimes admit.

Responsibility

As a society, we have given away our power to so-called authority figures for far too long. This is true in many avenues of our lives, no less so in regard to the food we put in our bodies. So often, we depend on the latest internet news story to inspire us to try a new food or diet and then get frustrated and stressed out when new reports contradict the previous one. Many decide to follow a health guru and follow his or her dictums religiously (or not religiously enough), but when they don't reach the goals and level of health they desired, it's on to the next guru or doctor. If only finding perfect health were that easy. As if someone who barely knows you, or who has possibly never met you, could determine the ideal methods for balancing your health.

Following the advice of gurus, reading books and articles, and attending lectures and seminars *can* get you quite far. These can serve to educate you on the options that are available and to new ideas; but in the end, the only expert on you is you! Once we take responsibility for our own health and begin the process of listening to our bodies and our intuition, in addition to the experts, we may begin to reach our loftiest health goals. We must educate our minds, feed our bodies, notice the results, adapt, and repeat.

Consciousness

We don't advocate that everyone lives exactly as we do. But we do advocate living according to principles. Your *own* principles. Our principles and how they relate to what we eat is one of the biggest ways in which we interact with the world. The decisions we make about our food have some of the most consistent and far-reaching effects of any in our daily lives.

For us to go on living, *something* must be consumed. Therefore, we must all make decisions about what we shall consume and in what quantities. If we wish to be conscious consumers, we should strongly consider how our choices will impact ourselves, our society, and the very planet we live on. All of which are intrinsically connected.

Attempting to cajole everyone into adhering to the same moral food code is not something we're interested in. Living consciously means adopting your own codes of conduct, attempting to live by them, being aware when individual choices are not consistent with your principles, and what effect those choices have. How can we make conscious choices without at least partially understanding the direct and indirect effects those choices have on ourselves, the planet, and the other beings we share the planet with? We must also be willing to adapt our principles as new information, ideas, and facts are uncovered.

To be conscious about food requires simply that we maintain constant moment-to-moment awareness about our choices. We are in fact the new hunter-gatherers. We have a diverse world in front of us and daily decisions to make that affect not just ourselves but the survival of the whole tribe.

Compassion

We have called raw vegan eating the *ahimsa* diet on many occasions. Loosely translated, it means "no-harm diet." We are clear that we want to cause as little suffering as possible. But remembering that the global food chain is complex and that humans are consummate consumers means realizing that our actions can still cause unintended harm.

Is there such a thing as a "zero emission" diet? Possibly, if you live on your own biodynamic farm. The majority of us, however, live in urban areas or at least rely on some portion of our food to come from elsewhere. Being honest about our consumption is an important key to making compassionate choices.

We also strive to be compassionate to ourselves. If we make the best choices we can, according to our principles, then we should treat ourselves kindly. We might make different decisions tomorrow if we are provided with new information, but knowing that we did our best with what we had today, and that we'll continue to do so, is freeing. Life is challenging for all of us at times. Treating ourselves, our neighbors, and the creatures with whom we share the planet to regular compassion is one of the best things we can do to make it a little easier.

Enjoyment

We love great tasting food. Food has evolved to a level of enjoyment previously unknown in human history. It has gone way beyond mere fuel for the body and has become a social pleasure, an art form, and a component of relaxation.

We don't advocate locking yourself away and sprouting in isolation because you don't know any other raw foodists. We believe in the healing power of sharing food with friends and family. If they don't always want to share in a raw meal, then occasionally you may find more benefit and enjoyment in joining them at a restaurant that can somewhat accommodate everyone's choices. You will likely find others at your table admiring your ability to find true enjoyment in simpler, more healthful fare.

The question is not if we will be extremists, but what kind of extremists we will be. The nation and the world are in dire need of creative extremists.

—Martin Luther King, Jr.

By being social and flexible, your friends and family will feel more at ease with your choices and may even end up approaching you with questions or asking for advice. By showing them that the raw food lifestyle is not an all-or-nothing commitment, they will be more interested in incorporating aspects into their own lives. Often when we have attended family holiday gatherings, we bring a raw dish to share. It prompts great discussion and usually ends up being completely eaten before we even get a chance to have some ourselves!

Being with those we love has a nutritional component and just feels good. Make whatever food adaptations you are comfortable with in those moments and simply enjoy being among good people. We eat healthfully so we'll have a long, enjoyable life. Without friends and family to share it with, it would just be a long life! And to let you in on one of our secrets: The more food we share with friends and family and the more we show ourselves to be supportive of the food choices of others, the more they seem to start eating and enjoying raw foods. That's the power of raw food—without the trappings of dogma or force it has the power to convince people on its own, one amazing bite at a time!

How to Use This Book

Eutrophology (ū'tro-fŏl' o-jy), n. A treatise on the art and science of elegant unfired table service; a literary work that treats of the wholesomeness and dainty preparation of the unfired diet; a treatise on, or a course in, the art of Eutrophing or elegant trophing which is the foundation of Trophotherapy and Trophoprophylactics; a discourse on Apyrtrophism.

—term coined by George Julius Drews, 1912

The legend that appears on each recipe page tells you, at a glance, what is involved in preparing each dish. This key allows you to decide "what to make for lunch" without having to read the whole book first!

Complexity

The first part of the key will be a number—1, 2, or 3—indicating the recipe's relative level of complexity. While none of these recipes is difficult to make, some are simpler than others. Below, you'll find a short description of what each number involves, and what each equipment icon symbolizes.

1 These recipes are the easiest to prepare because they contain fewer ingredients, require less equipment, or take less time to make. Although some of the recipes in this category have lengthy ingredient lists, often you will need only to put them in a blender and turn it on.

2 These may require more than one appliance or incorporate a greater number of steps.

3 These may depend upon more appliances, require more time to create, or involve subrecipes and/or some soaking and dehydrating.

Equipment Icons

B	**D**	**P**	**I**	**J**
High-speed blender	Food dehydrator	Food processor	Ice cream maker	Juicer

Learn more about these appliances in the Glossary on page 268.

THE RAWVOLUTION CONTINUES PLAYLIST

If you find yourself needing some great music to listen to while making recipes from this book, you may want to check out some of the following songs. This *RAWvolution Continues* playlist contains songs you're likely familiar with and some we're sure you'll be happy to discover. Some of these selections were written or performed by ELR customers or former employees, or by RAWvolutionaries of the past. Some of these tunes have provided the names for dishes in this collection of recipes, and others are important to us for other reasons. Enjoy!

Sweet Black Magic – Ryan Adams

Nature Boy – eden ahbez

Radio Euphoria – Joseph Arthur

Long Haired Child – Devendra Banhart

Revolution – The Beatles

Five Days in May – Blue Rodeo

Free Me – Cipes and the People

Do You Love Me – The Contours

Hanuman Chaleesa – Krishna Das

Jennifer Juniper – Donovan

The Revolution Starts Now – Steve Earle

My Sweet Lord – George Harrison

The Shining Hour – Grant Lee Buffalo

Cinnamon Love – The Jayhawks

Your Song – Elton John

Peace – Luminaries (feat. I,Star and Maesyn)

Woodstock – Joni Mitchell

Topanga Cowgirl – Mudcrutch

Californication – Red Hot Chili Peppers

If You See California – Chris Robinson

gandhi – Patti Smith

Children of the Revolution – T. Rex

Oh! Sweet Nuthin' – The Velvet Undergound

Lights – Victoria Williams

I'm Gonna Take You Home – Yahowa 13

Stocking Your Raw Kitchen

If the following list seems daunting, imagine how daunting creating anything but a salad was in the dark ages (pre-2003), before many of these products were easily available! Don't feel like you need to have *everything* on this list before you can begin experimenting with recipes. However, as these ingredients are nonperishable, why not stock up? The more complete your list is, the more options you'll have. All the items can be found at your local health food store or purchased online.

If you're unfamiliar with any items listed here, refer to the Glossary on page 268.

Regarding appliances, be sure, when purchasing a food dehydrator, to choose one with an adjustable thermostat that allows you to control the temperature.

OILS (LOOK FOR ORGANIC, COLD-PRESSED)

Coconut oil	Pumpkin seed oil
Flax oil	Sesame oil
Olive oil (stone-pressed)	

NUTS (LOOK FOR ORGANIC, RAW, UNSALTED)

Almonds	Jungle peanuts
Cashews	Pine nuts
Hazelnuts	Walnuts

SEEDS (LOOK FOR ORGANIC, RAW, UNSALTED)

Chia seeds	Sesame seeds (brown and black)
Flaxseeds	Sunflower seeds
Hemp seeds	

NUT AND SEED BUTTERS (LOOK FOR ORGANIC, RAW)

Almond butter	Jungle peanut butter
Cacao butter	Tahini
Coconut butter	

SEAWEED (LOOK FOR WILD OR ORGANIC)

Arame

Dulse flakes or granules

Dulse, whole-leaf

Irish moss

Kelp noodles

Nori (raw nori is black,
toasted nori is green)

Sea lettuce

Wakame

SPICES AND HERBS (LOOK FOR ORGANIC)

Allspice

Ancho chile powder

Black pepper, ground and peppercorns

Cayenne

Chili powder

Cinnamon

Cloves, ground and whole

Coriander, ground

Cumin, ground and whole seeds

Curry powder

Dill

Garam masala

Juniper berries

Nutmeg, ground and whole

Oregano

Paprika

Porcini mushroom powder

Red chile peppers (crushed)

Rosemary

Sage

Sea salt or Himalayan pink salt

Thyme

Turmeric

SUPERFOODS (LOOK FOR ORGANIC, RAW, WHEN AVAILABLE)

Açaí powder (look for freeze-dried)

Bee pollen (look for local)

Cacao powder (look for raw)

Cacao nibs

Chlorophyll (liquid)

Dr. Schulze's SuperFood Plus
powder

E3 Live, liquid blue-green algae

Goji berries

Goldenberries

Green powder

Hemp protein powder

Lucuma powder

Maca powder

Matcha green tea powder

Mesquite powder

Mulberries (dried)

Pomegranate powder

Purple corn powder

Reishi mushroom powder

Spirulina

Tocotrienols

SWEETENERS (LOOK FOR ORGANIC, RAW, WHEN AVAILABLE)

Coconut nectar

Coconut sugar

Stevia (liquid extract)

Yacon syrup

OTHER FOODS (LOOK FOR ORGANIC)

Apple cider vinegar (look for raw, unfiltered)

Buckwheat groats

Capers

Coconut (raw, shredded)

Coconut aminos (look for raw)

Dried strawberries (look for unsweetened)

Kombucha

Miso

Nutritional yeast

Olives, green and black (look for sun dried olives, cured in sea salt)

Peppermint essential oil

Probiotics

Pure water (spring or reverse osmosis)

Raisins

Stone-ground mustard

Tomatoes, sun dried

Teeccino herbal coffee (hazelnut flavor)

Thai coconut, water and flesh

Ume vinegar

Vanilla bean powder

Yerba mate

APPLIANCES

Vitamix, or other, high-speed blender

Food dehydrator (with thermostat)

Food processor

Ice cream maker

Juicer

TOOLS

Chocolate molds (polycarbonate)

Citrus juicer

Cutting board

Garlic press

Ice cream scoop, lever-style (1 oz.)

Knives, chef's and serrated

Mandolin slicer

Nut milk bag

Pastry bag

Spatula

Teflex sheets

Recipes

Fundamental Recipes

These recipes are the essentials, the foundations that are called for in so many dishes that appear in this book. Be sure to make extra so you can use them in multiple recipes, experiment with your own creations, or just stock up for the future!

Almond Milk

 B

MAKES 8 CUPS MILK OR APPROXIMATELY ¾ CUP PULP

7 cups coconut water　　　　　　　　**1 cup raw almonds**

In a high speed blender, combine the coconut water and almonds. Blend until smooth. Strain through a nut milk bag or cheesecloth to remove the almond pulp. Refrigerate the almond pulp for use in recipes for up to 4 days.

If you need to save the pulp for longer than 4 days, dehydrate the pulp for 24 hours and store it in a cool, dry place. If you used dehydrated almond pulp in any dishes, make sure to compensate with additional water as the recipes are designed to be used with freshly made pulp.

VARIATION: Make any type of nut milk you prefer using this simple recipe. Simply replace the almonds with any nuts or seeds.

Use almond pulp in the following dishes: **Cinnamon Raisin Bagels** (page 48), **Cinnamon Love French Toast** (page 51), **Focaccia Bread** (page 125), **Rosemary Crackers** (page 131), **Pesto Bruschetta** (page 129), **Bagel Sandwiches** (page 167), **Deep Dish Spinach Pizza** (page 173), **Vegetable Casserole** (page 206), **Black and White Cookies** (page 227)

Almond Milk is used in the following recipes: **Chia Porridge** (page 47), **Sprouted Buckwheat Granola** (page 65), **Über Protein Shake** (page 63), **Chai Shake** (page 35), **Almond Butter Shake** (page 34), **Sweet Green Smoothie** (page 66), **Spirulina Warrior Shake** (page 62), **Banana Yogurt Chi Shake** (page 40), **Durian Love Shake** (page 52), **Chocolate Durian Shake** (page 53), **Electrolyte Lemonade** (page 75), **Hot Chocolate** (page 82), **Motown Miracle** (page 83), **Wake Up Kiss** (page 95), **Sweet Black Magic Iced Coffee** (page 90), **Chai Latte** (page 71), **Green Tea Latte** (page 79), **Cream of Asparagus Soup** (page 104), **Cream of Carrot Soup** (page 104), **Hazelnut Mocha Shake** (page 53), **Nana-choco-squiter** (page 217), **Decadent Velvet Hot Chocolate** (page 241), **Chocolate Ganache Torte** (page 231), **Chai Spider Ice Cream Float** (page 240)

Basic Chocolate

....

MAKES 4½ CUPS

- **1 cup cacao butter**
- **2½ cups cacao powder**
- **1 cup coconut nectar**

- **1 tablespoon vanilla bean powder**
- **Pinch of sea salt**

Melt the cacao butter by placing it in a dish surrounded by hot water or in your dehydrator. Blend the melted cacao butter with the cacao powder, coconut nectar, vanilla bean powder, and salt in a high speed blender. Use while warm to make chocolates or as a sauce.

VARIATION: Add an extra ½ cup of cacao powder for darker chocolate.

Basic Chocolate is used in the following recipes: **Motown Miracle** (page 83), **Black and White Cookies** (page 227), **Dark Chocolate Peanut Butter Bars** (page 238), **Banana Lickety Split** (page 226), **Chocolate Ice Cream** (page 232), **Chocolate Buckwheat Tortugas** (page 228), **Montelimat Espresso Bonbons** (page 244) **Peppermint Patties** (page 248) **Almond Butter Cups** (page 224), **Mint Chocolate Hearts** (page 254)

Blue Corn Chips

....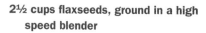

MAKES ABOUT 90 CHIPS

- **2½ cups flaxseeds, ground in a high speed blender**
- **2½ cups blue corn, ground in a high speed blender**
- **½ cup coconut aminos**
- **3 cups pure water**
- **¾ cup fresh lemon juice**

- **½ cup olive oil**
- **½ cup chopped stemmed cilantro**
- **1 tablespoon ground cumin**
- **1½ tablespoons sea salt**
- **½ teaspoon ground cayenne**
- **2 cloves garlic, peeled**

In a high speed blender, combine all of the ingredients and blend until smooth. Spread a thin layer onto a dehydrator tray lined with a Teflex sheet. Dehydrate one side at 105°F for approximately 14 hours. Flip onto a second dehydrator tray, peel off the Teflex sheet. Score the mixture twice horizontally and twice vertically to create 9 squares. Score each square in an "X" pattern to create triangle shapes. Dehydrate for an additional 12 to 14 hours. Store in a cool, dry place.

Blue Corn Chips are used in the following recipes: **Big Nachos** (page 117), **Hungry-Man Avocado Cheese Scramble** (page 57)

Burger Patties

MAKES 8 PATTIES

1½ cups raw walnuts, soaked for 3 to 4 hours and drained

¾ cup raw almonds, soaked for 3 to 4 hours and drained

¾ cup raw sunflower seeds, soaked for 3 to 4 hours and drained

1¼ cups chopped portobello mushrooms, briefly marinated in 2 to 3 tablespoons coconut aminos

1½ cups diced celery

¾ cup flaxseeds, ground in a high speed blender

½ yellow onion, diced

½ cup coconut aminos

¼ cup chopped stemmed parsley

5 cloves garlic, minced

3 tablespoons olive oil

2 tablespoons dried rosemary

1 tablespoon whole cumin seeds

¼ teaspoon cayenne

Using a food processor, grind the walnuts, almonds, and sunflower seeds. Transfer to a mixing bowl, add the remaining ingredients, and mix thoroughly, making sure to break apart any lumps.

Form the mixture by hand into round patties approximately ½ inch thick and 2¾ inches in diameter.

Dehydrate on a dehydrator tray lined with a Teflex sheet for 12 hours at 105°F. Flip the tray over onto an empty dehydrator tray and gently peel the Teflex sheet off the patties. Return to the dehydrator for another 20 hours. Store in a cool, dry place.

Burger Patties are used in the following recipes: **Mediterranean Burgers** (page 184), **Sprouted Black Bean Chili** (page 109), **Mushroom Swiss Burgers** (page 192)

Cream Cheese

MAKES 3½ CUPS

3 cups raw cashews

¼ cup apple cider vinegar

¼ cup fresh lemon juice

2 teaspoons sea salt

In a high speed blender, combine all of the ingredients and blend until smooth. Add a small amount of pure water if necessary to get a smooth consistency. If necessary, blend in 2 or 3 batches to make it easier to blend. Refrigerate until ready to serve.

Cream Cheese is used in the following recipes: **Cucumber Summer Rolls** (page 122), **Bagel Sandwiches** (page 167), **Santorini Sandwiches** (page 208), **Buddha-Bites Wontons** (page 118)

Faux Egg

MAKES 4 CUPS

1½ cups raw cashews

1 cup Irish Moss Gel (see sidebar, page 29)

1½ cups warm pure water

2 tablespoons fresh lemon juice

1 tablespoon turmeric

In a high speed blender, combine all of the ingredients and blend until smooth. Pour into a shallow pan, cover and refrigerate. Allow Faux Egg to sit overnight before use to ensure a more solid consistency.

Faux Egg is used in the following recipes: **Breakfast Burritos** (page 44), **Hungry-Man Avocado Cheese Scramble** (page 57), **Pad Thai** (page 195)

Garlic Cream Dressing

1 **B**

MAKES ABOUT 2 CUPS

¼ cup fresh lemon juice

¼ cup coconut aminos

8 cloves garlic, peeled

3-inch piece fresh ginger, peeled

1¼ cups olive oil

In a high speed blender, combine the lemon juice, coconut aminos, garlic, and ginger. While the blender is running, add the olive oil slowly in a stream until the dressing thickens and emulsifies (you may not need the full 1¼ cups of oil).

Garlic Cream Dressing is used in the following recipes: **Café Salad** (page 140), **Mushroom Swiss Burgers** (page 192), **Green Dragon Rolls** (page 176), **Californication Rolls** (page 169)

Guacamole

.... 1

MAKES ABOUT 5 CUPS

3 medium avocados, peeled

1 cup chopped green onions

1 bunch cilantro, stemmed and chopped

1 cup chopped tomatoes

¼ cup fresh lemon or lime juice

2 tablespoons olive oil

3 or 4 cloves garlic, minced

1 teaspoon sea salt

Combine all of the ingredients in a mixing bowl, mix well, and serve.

Guacamole is used in the following recipes: **Big Nachos** (page 117), **Taco Salad** (page 162), **Mexican Pizzas** (page 185), **Mole Tacos** (page 186)

Herbal Iced Coffee Concentrate

.... 1

MAKES 4 CUPS

3 Teeccino herbal coffee bags, hazelnut or preferred flavor

4 cups hot water

In a large glass jar, steep the bags in the hot water until cooled to room temperature. Store in the refrigerator until use.

Herbal Iced Coffee Concentrate is used in the following recipes: **Hazelnut Mocha Shake** (page 53), **Sweet Black Magic Iced Coffee** (page 90)

Mayo

 **1** **B**

MAKES ABOUT 5 CUPS

2 cups raw cashews

1½ cups coconut water

¾ cup fresh lemon juice

½ cup stone-ground mustard

5 cloves garlic, peeled

2 teaspoons sea salt

In a high speed blender, combine all of the ingredients and blend until smooth. Refrigerate until ready to serve.

Mayo is used in the following recipes: **Cheese-Stuffed Jalapeños** (page 121), **Taquitos with Paprika Sauce** (page 135), **Sea Cakes with Cilantro Chutney** (page 132), **Taco Salad** (page 162), **Cocophoria Sandwiches** (page 170), **Mock Chicken Sandwiches** (page 189), **Mock Turkey Sandwiches** (page 190), **Mole Tacos** (page 186), **Pesto Pizzas** (page 193), **Green Enchiladas** (page 178), **Mexican Pizzas** (page 185)

Nofu

 2 **B**

MAKES 4 CUPS

Nofu is incredibly versatile. Cut it into large cubes for a tofu substitute, small scoops to replace mozzarella, or crumbled to use as feta.

1½ cups raw cashews

1 cup Irish Moss Gel (see sidebar)

1½ cups warm pure water

2 tablespoons fresh lemon juice

In a high speed blender, combine all of the ingredients and blend until smooth. Pour into a shallow pan, cover, and refrigerate. Allow the Nofu to set up overnight before use to ensure a more solid consistency.

Nofu is used in the following recipes: **Warm Miso Soup** (page 113), **Holy Macro Bowl** (page 181), **Greek Salad with Cashew Feta** (page 145), **Mediterranean Burgers** (page 184)

IRISH MOSS GEL

Irish Moss Gel is made by soaking Irish moss overnight then blending with water. Soak 1 cup Irish moss in 2 cups pure water and let soak overnight. In the morning, drain the moss and rinse repeatedly until the seaweed smell is gone. In a high speed blender, combine and blend 2 cups soaked and rinsed Irish moss and 1½ cups pure water until a smooth clear gel is formed. Store, refrigerated, until needed.

RAWvolution's Famous Onion Bread

MAKES 9 SANDWICH-SIZE PIECES

The original raw Onion Bread recipe was created by Matt in 2002. Onion Bread has since become one of the most popular recipes in the raw food world.

3 large yellow onions

¾ cup flaxseeds, ground in a high speed blender

¾ cup sunflower seeds, ground in a food processor

½ cup coconut aminos

⅓ cup olive oil

Peel and halve the onions. In a food processor, cut the onions with the slicing disc. Transfer the cut onions to a large mixing bowl, add the remaining ingredients, and mix until thoroughly combined.

Spread 2 cups of the mixture evenly on a dehydrator tray lined with a Teflex sheet. Repeat until all of the mixture is used; more than one tray may be required. Dehydrate at 105°F for 24 hours. Flip the bread onto a second dehydrator tray, peel off the Teflex sheet, and dehydrate for an additional 12 to 14 hours. Once dehydrated, cut into 9 equal pieces (make 2 cuts horizontally and 2 cuts vertically).

RAWvolution's Famous Onion Bread is used in the following recipes: **Cocophoria Sandwiches** (page 170), **Mock Chicken Sandwiches** (page 189), **Mock Turkey Sandwiches** (page 190), **Mushroom Swiss Burgers** (page 192), **Santorini Sandwiches** (page 208), **Vegetable Casserole** (page 206), **Reuben Sandwiches** (page 198), **Mediterranean Burgers** (page 184), **Pesto Pizzas** (page 193), **Spicy Chipotle Burgers** (page 200)

Pesto

MAKES ABOUT 6 CUPS

2½ cups raw walnuts

3 bunches basil, stemmed

¼ cup olive oil

2 tablespoons fresh lemon juice, plus more for storing the pesto

2 teaspoons sea salt

Grind the walnuts in a food processor, slowly adding in the basil, olive oil, lemon juice, and sea salt. Pulse until well puréed. Refrigerate, with extra lemon juice squeezed on the top to prevent oxidation, until ready to serve.

Pesto is used in the following recipes: **Pesto Pizzas** (page 193), **Pesto Tomato Sliders** (page 129), **Pesto Bruschetta** (page 129)

Salsa

.... 1

MAKES ABOUT 3½ CUPS

2 cups diced tomatoes

¾ cup stemmed cilantro, chopped

½ cup chopped green onions

2 tablespoons fresh lemon or lime juice

1 tablespoon olive oil

4 cloves garlic, minced

1½ teaspoons ground cumin

¼ teaspoon ground cayenne

½ teaspoon sea salt

Combine all of the ingredients in a mixing bowl, mix well, and serve.

Salsa is used in the following recipes: **Breakfast Burritos** (page 44), **Hungry-Man Avocado Cheese Scramble** (page 57), **Big Nachos** (page 117), **Taco Salad** (page 162), **Mexican Pizzas** (page 185)

Seed Cheese

....

MAKES ABOUT 4 CUPS

½ cup fresh lemon juice

½ cup coconut aminos

4 or 5 cloves garlic, peeled

2¾ cups raw sunflower seeds, finely ground in a food processor (makes 3½ cups)

In a high speed blender, combine all of the ingredients, adding the ground sunflower seeds last. Blend thoroughly until the resulting cheese is very smooth and uniform.

Seed Cheese is used in the following recipes: **Hungry-Man Avocado Cheese Scramble** (page 57), **Cheese-Stuffed Jalapeños** (page 121), **Big Nachos** (page 117), **Mushroom Swiss Burgers** (page 192), **Mole Tacos** (page 186), **Taco Salad** (page 162)

Taco Meat

MAKES ABOUT 4½ CUPS

4 cups raw walnuts, ground in a food
processor

⅓ cup coconut aminos

4 teaspoons ground cumin

1½ teaspoons ground coriander

Combine all of the ingredients in a mixing bowl, mix well, and serve.

Taco Meat is used in the following recipes: **Big Nachos** (page 117), **Taco Salad** (page 162), **Mexican Pizzas** (page 185), **Taquitos with Paprika Sauce** (page 135), **Mole Tacos** (page 186), **Green Enchiladas** (page 178)

Yellow Wraps

MAKES 4 WRAPS

6 cups fresh coconut meat

¼ cup coconut aminos

¼ cup olive oil

¼ cup fresh lemon juice

1 tablespoon curry powder

2 pinches cayenne

1 teaspoon sea salt

In a high speed blender, combine all of the ingredients and blend until smooth. Spread the mixture thinly onto a dehydrator tray lined with a Teflex sheet. Dehydrate at 105°F for 12 to 14 hours. Flip the bread onto a second dehydrator tray, peel off the Teflex sheet, and dehydrate for an additional 4 hours. Cut into 4 equal squares. Store in a cool, dry place.

Yellow Wraps are used in the following recipes: **Taquitos with Paprika Sauce** (page 135), **Buddha-Bites Wontons** (page 118), **Tiger Rolls** (page 205)

Breakfasts, Shakes, & Smoothies

Breakfast has always been a favorite meal in our house. It's the time of day when we are most clear about our intention to eat healthy, powerful foods. For us, that often means a superfood smoothie, especially on days when we have a lot planned. Superfood smoothies are great because you can pour all of the things you know are good for you into one blender and enjoy it all morning long. That's how the M&J Ultimate Shake was invented! After a drink like that, you'll have great energy for the rest of the day and the satisfaction of knowing that you gave yourself a terrific start! Some days, of course, you might just crave French toast or pancakes. Either way—we've got you covered.

Almond Butter Shake

MAKES 2 SERVINGS

Two delicious ice cream shakes, two amazing and unique flavors.

2¼ cups nut milk (see Almond Milk, page 24)

4 scoops Vanilla Ice Cream (page 235)

¼ cup raw almond butter

4 ice cubes

In a high speed blender, combine all of the ingredients and blend until smooth. Serve immediately.

RAWVOLUTIONARY HERO

Pythagoras, an eminent Greek philosopher, also made influential contributions to religious teaching in the late 6th century BCE. He is revered as a mathematician, mystic, and scientist. According to Diogenes Laërtius, respected biographer of the Greek philosophers, Pythagoras insisted that his disciples become *apuratrophists* and eat their food *apura* or "unfired."

Chai Shake

② B I

MAKES 2 SERVINGS

1½ cups nut milk (see Almond Milk,
    page 24)

4½ tablespoons coconut butter

2 tablespoons coconut nectar

2½ tablespoons grated or minced peeled
    fresh ginger

2 teaspoons cinnamon

½ teaspoon ground black pepper

½ teaspoon grated nutmeg

½ teaspoon ground cardamom

¼ teaspoon vanilla bean powder

¼ teaspoon ground cloves

3 scoops Vanilla Ice Cream (page 235)

8 ice cubes

In a high speed blender, combine all of the ingredients and blend until smooth.
Serve immediately.

RAWVOLUTIONARY HEROES

The Essenes were an ancient sect of Judaism who are commonly believed to have authored the famed Dead Sea Scrolls. *The Essene Gospel of Peace,* a book discovered at the Vatican and translated from ancient Aramaic, quotes Jesus as having said, "If you eat living food, the same will quicken you, but if you kill your food, the dead food will kill you also. For life comes only from life, and from death comes always death."

Aztec Maca Shake

MAKES 3 SERVINGS

Our quintessential chocolate shake, sweetened only with coconut water, is good for an everyday pick-me-up. Maca is an unrivaled Peruvian superfood that, combined with cacao, gives you balanced energy for hours.

3½ cups coconut water

2 cups fresh coconut meat

⅓ cup cacao powder

2 tablespoons maca powder

2 tablespoons mesquite powder

In a high speed blender, combine all of the ingredients and blend until smooth. Serve chilled.

NOTE: Some folks would prefer this drink to be sweeter. If that's you, feel free to add some coconut nectar or another raw sweetener.

RAWVOLUTIONARY HERO

Sylvester Graham, inventor of the graham cracker (ironically), recommended "unfired" vegetables and fruits as the optimum diet. In 1839 he wrote that humans would never suffer illness if they ate only uncooked foods. In his 1849 book, *Lectures on the Science of Human Life,* Graham wrote: "All cooked food, even under the best regulations, impairs in some degree the power of the stomach to digest . . ."

Apple Bread

MAKES 9 PIECES

A non-savory take on our famous Onion Bread (page 30), this sweet bread is chewy and delicious. It's great spread with coconut oil, nut butter, or even both!

5 cups shredded cored apples

½ cup flaxseeds, ground in a high speed blender

½ cup sunflower seeds, ground in a food processor

4 teaspoons coconut nectar

1 teaspoon ground cinnamon

In a large mixing bowl, combine all of the ingredients and mix well by hand. Spread approximately 2 cups of the mixture evenly on a dehydrator tray lined with a Teflex sheet. Repeat until all of the mixture is used.

Dehydrate one side at 105°F for approximately 14 hours. Flip the bread onto a second dehydrator tray, peel off the Teflex sheet, and dehydrate for an additional 12 to 14 hours. Once dehydrated, cut into 9 equal pieces (make 2 cuts horizontally and 2 cuts vertically).

Store in a dry place.

RAWVOLUTIONARY HERO

Louis Kuhne, a German naturopath, published *New Science of Healing* in 1883. In it he writes: "Food precisely in the form nature gives it to us, is always the best for the digestion," and "Man is a frugivorous animal." On the works of Louis Kuhne (and Adolf Just), Mahatma Gandhi remarked, "It is our duty to read them."

Banana Yogurt Chi Shake

MAKES 1 SERVING

We blended our yummy coconut yogurt with bananas, figs, and maca to whip up this quick and delicious breakfast drink.

¾ cup Tangy Coconut Yogurt (page 68)

¾ cup nut milk (see Almond Milk, page 24)

½ banana

2 dried figs

1 teaspoon lucuma powder

1 teaspoon tocotrienols

1 teaspoon maca powder

½ teaspoon ground cinnamon

In a high speed blender, combine all of the ingredients and blend until smooth. Serve chilled.

RAWVOLUTIONARY HERO

Adolf Just was a German naturopath who counted Franz Kafka and Mahatma Gandhi as fans. In his 1896 book, *Return to Nature!,* Just wrote: "A diet of raw fruit does very much to increase all the powers of the body, and still more, all the original higher spiritual capacities and god-like faculties of man."

Breakfast Bread

MAKES 2 LARGE LOAVES

A recipe created by raw pastry chef Krisztina Agramonte. Next to the M&J Ultimate Shake (page 54), this is my all-time favorite breakfast! —Matt

1 cup mulberries, ground in a food
  processor

1½ cups coconut sugar, ground in a food
  processor

8 bananas

3 cups pure water

½ cup ground cinnamon

4 cups whole flaxseeds, ground in a high
  speed blender, plus more if needed

2½ cups raisins

2 cups chopped raw walnuts

1 cup whole mulberries

Combine the ground mulberries and coconut sugar in a bowl and mix well. Set aside ½ cup to top the loaves.

In a blender, combine the bananas, water, and cinnamon and blend well.

In a large mixing bowl, combine the ground mulberry mixture, the banana mixture, and the ground flaxseeds and mix well. Fold in the raisins, chopped walnuts, and whole mulberries. Knead until all liquid is absorbed by the dry ingredients and a doughy texture is achieved. Let the mixture sit for 20 to 30 minutes if necessary until the water has been absorbed completely. If the mixture is still runny, knead in a small amount of ground flaxseeds to absorb the remaining liquid.

Form the dough into 2 large loaves. Make the loaves flatter than they are wide or long to allow them to dry properly. Pat the reserved ½ cup ground mulberries onto the outside of the loaves.

Place the loaves on a dehydrator tray lined with a Teflex sheet. Dehydrate the loaves at 105°F for about 24 hours. Look for the texture to be crispy on the outside and soft but not wet on the inside. Slice and serve.

VARIATIONS: Change up the flavors on this bread by adding any combination of poppy seeds, cacao powder, Herbal Iced Coffee Concentrate (page 28), cacao nibs, cashew or almond butter, or goji berries.

RAWVOLUTIONARY HERO

Maximilian Bircher-Benner is best known for inventing muesli cereal, though the Swiss physician used a diet of raw foods to heal patients at his Vital Force sanitarium in Zürich, which opened in 1904. Bircher-Benner believed that cooking destroys much of food's nutrients and theorized that because plants contain more of the sun's energy, they must be more nutritious than meat.

Breakfast Burritos

MAKES 4 BURRITOS

A gently spicy chipotle wrap stuffed with avocado, fresh salsa, and cashew egg.

FOR THE CHIPOTLE WRAPS

1 cup fresh coconut meat (see Note)

2 teaspoons ancho chile powder

1 teaspoon coconut aminos

1 teaspoon olive oil

1 teaspoon chipotle powder

1 teaspoon sea salt

⅔ teaspoon fresh lemon juice

½ teaspoon ground cumin

½ clove garlic, peeled

FOR THE FILLING

8 romaine lettuce leaves

1 avocado, sliced

2 cups Faux Egg (page 27)

¾ cup Salsa (page 31)

To make the wraps, in a high speed blender, combine all of the ingredients and blend until smooth. Spread the mixture very thinly on a dehydrator tray lined with a Teflex sheet. Dehydrate one side at 105°F for approximately 14 hours. Flip the bread onto a second dehydrator tray, peel off the Teflex sheet, and dehydrate for an additional 4 hours. Once dehydrated, cut into four equal pieces.

To fill the wraps, line each with 2 romaine leaves and one-fourth of the avocado slices, top each with one-fourth of the Faux Egg and the Salsa. Roll the wraps to close and firmly press to seal.

NOTE: If the coconut meat is on the dry side, add some pure water or coconut water to make a more spreadable consistency.

RAWVOLUTIONARY HERO

Bernarr Macfadden was internationally famous in his era. Macfadden ran several health sanitariums, owned many restaurants, was a bodybuilder and magnate in the publishing world, and authored over 100 books. In his 1901 book, *Strength from Eating*, Macfadden wrote, "It is easy to reason to the conclusion that a raw diet—grains, vegetables, fruits, and nuts—should be the natural food of man."

Chia Porridge

··· **1** **B**

MAKES 1 SERVING

This light but filling porridge is a healthy and hearty way to start your day. Chia is a complete superfood packed with essential fatty acids, fiber, and protein.

⅓ cup chia seeds

½ cup pure water

½ cup nut milk (see Almond Milk, page 24)

Dash of ground cinnamon

Coconut nectar or other sweetener, to taste

Soak the chia seeds in the water in a cereal bowl for 15 minutes or until gelatinous. Pour the nut milk over the chia seeds. Add the cinnamon and the sweetener to taste.

SERVING SUGGESTIONS: Add walnuts, bananas, strawberries, goji berries, dried mulberries, raisins, or anything else that sounds good.

Chia seeds were eaten by ancient and indigenous cultures such as the Aztecs and the Tarahumara to provide long-lasting energy during battles, hunts, and athletic competitions. Yes, they are the same seeds that grow chia pets.

RAWVOLUTIONARY HEROES

Eugene Christian and **Mollie Griswold Christian** threw a gala dinner party in 1903 in which all the dishes in an elaborate four-course meal were uncooked. They also wrote what is almost certainly the world's first raw food recipe book, *Uncooked Foods and How to Use Them,* in 1904.

Cinnamon Raisin Bagels

MAKES 8 SERVINGS

Chewy, with extra raisins, these sweet bagels are great for breakfast or as a snack. If you eat them warm, right out of the dehydrator, you'll be in instant cinnamon heaven!

2 cups flaxseeds, ground in a high speed blender

1 cup shredded peeled zucchini

1 cup almond pulp (see Almond Milk, page 24)

¾ cup raisins

¾ cup coconut nectar

2 teaspoons ground cinnamon

In a large mixing bowl, combine all of the ingredients. Knead the mixture by hand until a consistent, doughy texture is achieved. By hand, shape the dough into 8 bagels. If the dough becomes tacky, use a small amount of pure water or coconut oil to smooth it out. Place the bagels on a dehydrator tray and dehydrate at 105°F for 48 hours.

SERVING SUGGESTION: These bagels are delicious served with raw almond butter.

RAWVOLUTIONARY HEROES

Naturmenschen were a group of late 19th and early 20th century German and Swiss "Natural Men" who wore tunics and sandals (or bare feet), long hair, and beards and preferred to eat only uncooked foods. Karl Wilhelm Diefenbach, Johannes Guttzeit, Gustav Nagel, Ralph Salomonson, Josua Klein, Gusto Graser, the influential artist Fidus, and author Herman Hesse exemplified the *Naturmenschen* ideal.

Cinnamon Love French Toast

MAKES 4 TO 6 SERVINGS

I wanted to create a healthful version of my favorite Sunday morning breakfast. This unlikely combination of almonds, flax, and zucchini does the trick! —*Janabai*

2 cups shredded peeled zucchini

1 cup flaxseeds, ground in a high speed blender

1 cup almond pulp (see Almond Milk, page 24)

½ cup coconut nectar

2 tablespoons ground cinnamon

Cinnamon Nectar (below)

In a large mixing bowl, combine all of the ingredients except the Cinnamon Nectar and mix well by hand. Knead the mixture by hand until a consistent, doughy texture is achieved. Spread the mixture one-fourth inch thick on a dehydrator tray lined with a Teflex sheet.

Dehydrate one side at 105°F for approximately 14 hours. Flip the French toast onto a second dehydrator tray, peel off the Teflex sheet, and dehydrate for an additional 12 to 14 hours. Cut into 9 equal pieces (make 2 cuts horizontally and 2 cuts vertically), then cut the nine squares in half diagonally. Refrigerate until ready to serve. Drizzle the toast generously with the Cinnamon Nectar and serve.

Cinnamon Nectar

2 cups coconut nectar

3 tablespoons ground cinnamon

With a spoon or fork, thoroughly mix the coconut nectar and cinnamon.

RAWVOLUTIONARY HERO

Bill Pester left Germany at age 19 to avoid the draft and brought the *Naturmensch* ideals to the United States in 1906. Eventually settling in the mountains near Palm Springs, Pester was likely California's first hippie, preceding the flower children of the 1960s by several decades!

Durian Love Shake

MAKES 1 SERVING

The durian fruit is considered a traditional aphrodisiac. There's a saying in Indonesia: "When the durians come off the trees, the sarongs come off too!"

- **1 cup nut milk (see Almond Milk, page 24)**
- **1 cup seeded durian**
- **2 teaspoons ground cinnamon**

In a high speed blender, combine all of the ingredients and blend until smooth. Serve chilled.

NOTE: At a pool party one summer, we met a couple who told us they'd had their first Durian Love Shakes on their first date at ELR at my suggestion. They proceeded to tell me that they are now married. Hmmm . . . —*Janabai*

RAWVOLUTIONARY HERO

Horace Fletcher made a name for himself by arguing that food should be chewed 32 times before being swallowed. The Great Masticator, as he was known, also held that food should either be unfired or lightly cooked in order to give the teeth and jaw muscles an adequate workout. Upton Sinclair, Mark Twain, and John D. Rockefeller all tested his theories for themselves.

Chocolate Durian Shake

2 **B** **I**

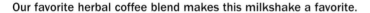

MAKES 1 SERVING

1 cup nut milk (see Almond Milk, page 24)

2 scoops Chocolate Ice Cream (page 232)

¾ cup seeded durian

1 tablespoon cacao powder

4 ice cubes

In a high speed blender, combine all of the ingredients and blend until smooth. Serve immediately.

Hazelnut Mocha Shake

2 **B** **I**

MAKES 1 SERVING

Our favorite herbal coffee blend makes this milkshake a favorite.

1 cup nut milk (see Almond Milk, page 24)

½ cup Herbal Iced Coffee Concentrate (page 28)

½ cup Chocolate Ice Cream (page 232)

1 tablespoon cacao powder

1 tablespoon almond butter

4 ice cubes

In a high speed blender, combine all of the ingredients and blend until smooth. Serve immediately.

RAWVOLUTIONARY HERO

Julian P. Thomas, author of *The Advantages of Raw Food* (1905), stated: "For ages animals who fed on raw food have had better health than man. The more people cook their food the more unhealthy they become."

M&J Ultimate Shake

 1 **B**

MAKES 2 SERVINGS

Chocolate, coconut, and more than a half-dozen other superfoods! It's so tasty, you won't believe it contains more nutrition than most people get in days!

- 1½ cups nut milk (see Almond Milk, page 24)
- 1 cup coconut water
- ½ cup fresh coconut meat
- ¼ cup goji berries
- ¼ cup bee pollen (optional)
- 1-ounce shot E3 Live
- 1 scoop (2 tablespoons) raw protein powder

- 3 tablespoons maca powder
- 2 tablespoons Billy's Infinity Greens powder or other green powder
- 2 tablespoons tocotrienols
- 1½ tablespoons cacao powder
- 1 tablespoon hemp or flax oil
- 1 tablespoon lucuma powder
- 2 teaspoons mesquite powder

In a high speed blender, combine all of the ingredients and blend together until smooth. Serve chilled.

RAWVOLUTIONARY HERO

Hereward Carrington, Ph.D., was a well-known British investigator and author on the subjects of psychic phenomena and alternative health in the first half of the 20th century. Dr. Carrington wrote extensively on fruitarianism and fasting, stating ". . . I shall endeavor to show that fruits and nuts in their uncooked, primitive form, are the suitable and proper diet for mankind."

Before the M&J was on the menu, customers would see Matt drinking the shake he made just for the two of us in the mornings and ask him what it was. He would explain that it wasn't a menu item and that it was just a custom drink he made that combined all of our favorite superfoods into one drink. He eventually had to give the recipe to the staff when customers began demanding the drink!

Hungry-Man
Avocado Cheese Scramble

2 **B**

MAKES 1 OR 2 SERVINGS

For the mornings when you're really hungry and want a hearty but healthful breakfast.

½ avocado, cubed

¾ cup Faux Egg (page 27), chopped

½ cup sliced mushrooms, marinated
    lightly in coconut aminos

½ red bell pepper, diced

2 tablespoons diced red onion

Combine all of the ingredients in a mixing bowl and mix together gently until evenly
distributed. Spoon the mixture onto plates and serve.

SERVING SUGGESTIONS: This scramble goes well with our Blue Corn Chips (page 25) and
Salsa (page 31).

RAWVOLUTIONARY HERO

O. L. M. Abramowski was a German
doctor and raw food enthusiast. In his
1908 book *Fruit Can Heal You!,* he wrote:
"Natural uncooked food has saved my life,
has rejuvenated my body and made out
of an overfed, old man, courting apoplexy
and rushing blindly into a premature
grave, a comparatively young, vigorous
and healthy person, fit and willing to live
another half century."

Oh! Sweet Nuthin' Pancakes

MAKES 2 OR 3 SERVINGS

Named after Matt's favorite Velvet Underground song, these chia seed pancakes are fun and nutritious, and the cinnamon coconut nectar syrup is sublime!

2¼ cups coconut water

2 cups raw cashews

¼ cup chia seeds, ground in a high speed blender

2 tablespoons coconut nectar

1 teaspoon ground cinnamon

Cinnamon Nectar (see Cinnamon Love French Toast, page 51)

In a high speed blender, combine all of the ingredients except the Cinnamon Nectar and blend until smooth. Pour silver dollar–size batter rounds onto a dehydrator tray lined with a Teflex sheet. Dehydrate on one side at 105°F for 12 to 14 hours. Flip the pancakes onto a second dehydrator tray, peel off the Teflex sheet, and dehydrate for an additional 4 hours. Refrigerate until served. Drizzle with the Cinnamon Nectar to serve.

SERVING SUGGESTION: Consider making them in the shape of the initial letter of your kids' names like my dad did with regular pancakes! —Matt

RAWVOLUTIONARY HERO

George Julius Drews called his 1912 system of curing disease using raw foods "Trophotherapy." On "unfired" foods, of which he wrote extensively, he said, "The Unfired diet is truly attractive, is moral, aesthetic, delicious and good . . .", and "Nature will do the curing if you will aid her by eating unfired food."

Mango Smoothie

MAKES 2 SERVINGS

There is nothing simpler or fresher tasting than these fruit smoothies combining fresh fruit and whole coconuts.

2 cups chopped pitted mango

1¼ cups fresh coconut meat

¾ cup coconut water

In a high speed blender, combine all of the ingredients and blend until smooth. Serve chilled.

Strawberry Smoothie

MAKES 2 SERVINGS

2 cups strawberries

1¼ cups fresh coconut meat

¾ cup coconut water

In a high speed blender, combine all of the ingredients and blend until smooth. Serve chilled.

RAWVOLUTIONARY HERO

Benedict Lust was a German doctor and one of the founders of naturopathic medicine. Lust regained his health after suffering from tuberculosis and later opened his Yungborn retreat and sanitarium in the United States. Lust's writings and magazines introduced America not only to German methods, but also to the Indian concepts of Ayurveda and yoga. In 1915, his book *Raw Food Table* was published.

Spirulina Warrior Shake

1 B

MAKES 1 SERVING

Tons of spirulina, raw protein powder, and coconut meat for this simple yet filling shake.

1¼ cups coconut water

½ cup fresh coconut meat

1 scoop (2 tablespoons) raw protein powder

1 teaspoon spirulina powder

1 teaspoon flax oil

In a high speed blender, combine all of the ingredients and blend until smooth. Serve chilled.

RAWVOLUTIONARY HERO

Arnold Ehret was a German health educator and the author of two classics in the raw foods canon: *The Mucusless Diet Healing System* (circa 1919) and *Rational Fasting* (circa 1921). Ehret claimed to have cured himself of kidney disease with his system of fasting and a predominantly raw vegetarian diet. Ehret is also known for healing clinics he ran in Europe and later in Los Angeles.

Über Protein Shake

1 **B**

MAKES 1 SERVING

This nutritious protein shake combines multiple proteins to form a drink so packed with protein even the guys at the gym will be impressed!

- **1¼ cups nut milk (see Almond Milk, page 24)**
- **1 scoop (2 tablespoons) Sunwarrior protein powder**
- **1 scoop (2 tablespoons) Raw Power protein powder**
- **1 scoop (2 tablespoons) Nutiva protein powder**

In a high speed blender, combine all of the ingredients and blend until smooth. Serve chilled.

NOTE: Feel free to use other raw protein powders of your choice.

VARIATION: Add a banana and cacao powder to make a fruity, chocolaty version.

Regarding the never-ceasing question of protein: Yes, there are many vegan-suitable plant proteins that are complete proteins! Very few people seem to suffer from protein deficiencies.

Sprouted Buckwheat Granola

2 D

MAKES 2 OR 3 SERVINGS

This breakfast granola combines crunchy sprouted buckwheat, raisins, and walnuts for a satisfying morning meal.

3 cups buckwheat, soaked for 40 to 60 minutes, drained and sprouted for 24 hours

1 cup raisins

¾ cup raw walnuts

2 tablespoons ground ground cinnamon

2 tablespoons coconut nectar

In a large mixing bowl, combine all of the ingredients and mix by hand. Spread the mixture onto a dehydrator tray. Dehydrate for 48 hours at 105°F, or until completely dry. Store in a cool, dry place.

SERVING SUGGESTION: Serve with the nut milk of your choice (see Almond Milk, page 24) and top with fresh berries.

RAWVOLUTIONARY HERO

Stella McDermott wrote in her 1919 book, *Metaphysics of Raw Foods*, "Why should we eat raw food? Because in its natural state it is full of life. . . . Cooking destroys the life."

Sweet Green Smoothie

MAKES 1 SERVING

This simple smoothie, packed with baby greens and spirulina, is great for breakfast.

1¼ cups nut milk (see Almond Milk, page 24)

1 cup baby greens

1 tablespoon tocotrienols

1 teaspoon spirulina powder

In a high speed blender, combine all of the ingredients and blend until smooth. Serve chilled.

RAWVOLUTIONARY HEROES

Vera Richter authored *Cook-Less Book,* which first appeared in print in 1925. Many attribute the widespread use of the phrase "raw fooder" to Vera, her husband, John, and their Los Angeles clientele. Indeed, the terms "raw fooder," "live foods," and "uncooked" are mentioned dozens of times throughout their books.

John Richter, author of *Nature—The Healer* (1936), owned and ran three restaurants from 1917 to 1942 that operated under the name the Eutropheon (Greek for "good nourishment"). These were Los Angeles', and likely the world's, very first raw food restaurants. Many of the Nature Boys were employed by, or were regulars at, the Eutropheon restaurants.

Tangy Coconut Yogurt

1 **B**

MAKES 4 TO 6 SERVINGS

Creamy and fluffy, this probiotic yogurt is so great that we just can't get enough of it—and neither can our customers. Some folks (and their children), like it so much they buy it two quarts at a time. Be sure to make enough!

7 cups fresh coconut meat
2 cups fresh lemon juice

4 capsules probiotics

In a high speed blender, combine all of the ingredients and blend until smooth. Pour the mixture into a large glass container and let sit covered at room temperature for 24 hours. Store the fermented yogurt in the refrigerator. Use 1 cup of fermented yogurt in place of the probiotics to start your next batch.

SERVING SUGGESTIONS: This yogurt is great with our Sprouted Buckwheat Granola (page 65) or simply topped with fresh fruit.

Drinks
& Elixirs

We all know that high-quality water
is the foundation of any healthy
lifestyle. Sometimes, though, eight
glasses of plain H_2O daily can get
a bit boring! To help, we present
18 amazing drinks—all fun, all
functional! These delicious drinks
are great for enlivening your day and
impressing your friends!

Chai Latte

MAKES 2 SERVINGS

We make this creamy chai with fresh cinnamon, cardamom, and nutmeg. It tastes great and has no caffeine!

2 cups hot water

¾ cup nut milk (see Almond Milk, page 24)

4½ tablespoons coconut butter

2½ tablespoons chopped peeled ginger

2 tablespoons coconut nectar

½ teaspoon ground black pepper

½ teaspoon grated nutmeg

½ teaspoon ground cardamom

¼ teaspoon vanilla bean powder

¼ teaspoon ground cloves

2 teaspoons grated cinnamon

In a high speed blender, combine all of the ingredients except the cinnamon and blend until smooth. Sprinkle with the cinnamon. Serve immediately.

RAWVOLUTIONARY HERO

Otto Carque was likely the first to use the term "natural foods" in business. In 1905, he began selling natural foodstuffs out of a truck he dubbed his "health wagon" and opened three health food shops in Los Angeles. In his 1923 book, *Rational Diet,* Carque wrote: "The *strictly vegetarian diet* will only prove satisfactory when it consists largely of uncooked foods to insure the full benefit derived from vitamins and organic salts."

Chlorophyll Lemonade

MAKES 2 SERVINGS

Chlorophyll is amazing. Almost identical to human blood molecules, it has the power to regenerate the body on a cellular level. Adding chlorophyll to lemonade is a simple and tasty way to get a dose daily.

½ cup fresh lemon juice

¼ cup liquid chlorophyll

2 tablespoons coconut nectar

2¼ cups pure water

Stir all of the ingredients together in a large container, or add the chlorophyll last, as pictured. Serve over ice.

RAWVOLUTIONARY HERO

James Faulkner, lecturer and author of the 1923 book, *The Unfired Food Diet Simplified,* stated: "Cook stove products are far less sustaining than unfired foods."

Electrolyte Lemonade

MAKES 1 SERVING

This recipe is our twist on David and Annie Jubbs' raw food classic. This tart but sweet drink replaces electrolytes, provides vitamin C for regeneration, and cleanses the liver and gall bladder.

¾ cup nut milk (see Almond Milk, page 24)

1 medium-size lemon, quartered (without rind, pith remaining; remove the outer yellow, keep the white layer that is directly underneath)

3 strawberries with their tops

1 tablespoon coconut nectar

1 tablespoon flax oil or coconut oil

1-inch piece peeled fresh ginger

In a high speed blender, combine all of the ingredients and blend until smooth. Serve chilled.

RAWVOLUTIONARY HERO

Johanna Brandt was a South African propagandist and a spy during the Boer War who smuggled information using letters written in invisible ink made from lemon juice. Her best-known publication, though, is 1927's *The Grape Cure.* In it, she states: "Every kitchen stove is a laboratory on which the living essence is converted into dead matter." In 2000, the South African Post Office honored Brandt with a stamp depicting her image.

Goji Lemonade

 1 **B**

MAKES 2 SERVINGS

We make goji juice straight from the antioxidant rich berries and add fresh ginger and lemon to create a refreshing summer drink.

4 cups pure water

1 cup goji berries

½ cup fresh lemon juice

¼ cup coconut nectar

1½-inch piece peeled fresh ginger

In a high speed blender, combine all of the ingredients and blend until smooth. Strain through a nut milk bag or cheesecloth to remove the ginger and goji berry pulp. Serve chilled.

RAWVOLUTIONARY HERO

St. Louis Estes was an American doctor who styled himself "the father and founder of the international back to nature raw foods movement." He so improved his health using raw foods that he began lecturing on the topic throughout the United States. His 1927 book, *Raw Food and Health,* is considered a raw food classic. In it, he writes: "Build the body on fresh raw foods which are vital and carry 100 per cent nutrition."

Green Tea Latte

● 1 ● B

MAKES 2 SERVINGS

Green tea is a super power herb and makes for a tasty flavor in this creamy beverage.

2 cups hot water

¾ cup nut milk (see Almond Milk, page 24)

4½ tablespoons coconut butter

2 tablespoons coconut nectar

2 teaspoons green tea powder

½ teaspoon vanilla bean powder

In a high speed blender, combine all of the ingredients and blend until smooth. Serve immediately.

RAWVOLUTIONARY HERO

E. L. Moraine Estes was a Doctor of Naturopathic Medicine, a Doctor of Chiropractic, and wife of Dr. St. Louis Estes. In her 1927 publication, *Raw Food Menu and Recipe Book,* she states that their eight children ". . . have never suffered from any of the illnesses common to childhood. . . . This is because they have been raised on uncooked foods, fruit and vegetable juices . . ."

Hawaiian Heat

 J

MAKES 3 SERVINGS

Pineapple juice and cayenne are a surprisingly delicious combination. We first had a version of this drink on our honeymoon in Maui.

1 medium-size pineapple, peeled and juiced

4-inch piece peeled fresh ginger, juiced

1¼ cups fresh lemon juice

½ teaspoon crushed red chile peppers

Combine all of the ingredients in a large pitcher and stir. Serve chilled.

RAWVOLUTIONARY HERO

Edmond Bordeaux Szekely was a Hungarian philologist, linguist, philosopher, and psychologist. Szekely claimed that while studying at the Vatican in 1923 he found and translated several obscure Hebrew and Aramaic texts which he said proved the Essenes were vegetarians, and that vegetarianism and raw foodism were prescribed by Jesus. The first texts were published as *The Essene Gospel of Peace* in 1928.

Hazelnut Horchata

MAKES 3 TO 4 SERVINGS

A spin on the traditional Mexican dessert drink made from hazelnuts.

¾ cup raw hazelnuts

4 cups coconut water

2 tablespoons lucuma powder

2 tablespoons coconut nectar

1½ tablespoons ground cinnamon

¼ teaspoon vanilla bean powder

In a high speed blender, blend the hazelnuts and coconut water together. Strain through a nut milk bag or cheesecloth to remove the hazelnut pulp. Return the mixture to the blender, add the remaining ingredients, and blend until smooth. Serve chilled.

RAWVOLUTIONARY HERO

Mohandas Gandhi is one of the most well-known and well-respected people in all of history. He led the nation of India to independence from British rule with his pioneering use of nonviolent civil disobedience. In 1929, Gandhi wrote: "As a searcher for truth I deem it necessary to find the perfect food for a man to keep body, mind, and soul in a sound condition. I believe that the search can only succeed with unfired food . . ."

Hot Chocolate

 1 **B**

MAKES 2 SERVINGS

Combining raw cacao, coconut butter, and almond milk, this sweet and creamy treat is
a lovely pick-me-up on a chilly day.

- 1 cup hot water
- ½ cup nut milk (see Almond Milk, page 24)
- 3½ tablespoons coconut butter

- 3½ tablespoons cacao powder
- 1 tablespoon coconut nectar
- ½ teaspoon vanilla bean powder

In a high speed blender, combine all of the ingredients and blend until smooth.
Serve immediately.

RAWVOLUTIONARY HERO

Paul Kouchakoff was a Swiss doctor who, in 1930, found that digestive leukocytosis, a stress response observed when the body is invaded by a dangerous pathogen and marked by the immediate increase in our white blood cell count, occurred when cooked foods were consumed. In his studies, digestive leukocytosis did not occur when plant foods were eaten in their natural, unheated state.

Motown Miracle

MAKES 2 SERVINGS

This one is for Berry Gordy. He loves raw vegan foods and ate at ELR for his 81st birthday. Janabai whipped up this drink for him on the spot.

1 cup nut milk (see Almond Milk, page 24)

1 cup coconut water

4 teaspoons cacao powder

4 teaspoons coconut nectar

1 teaspoon lucuma powder

Pinch of cinnamon

In a high speed blender, combine all of the ingredients and blend until smooth. Serve as is or over ice.

SERVING SUGGESTION: Chill the glass and dip the rim in chocolate sauce (see Basic Chocolate, page 25).

RAWVOLUTIONARY HERO

Herbert Shelton was an American alternative medicine advocate, author, pacifist, and supporter of raw foodism and fasting. He revitalized the 1800s approach to healing known as the Natural Hygiene method in the 1920s and went on to found the American Natural Hygiene Society in 1948. In 1956, Shelton was nominated by the American Vegetarian Party to run as its candidate for President of the United States.

No-Egg Nog

MAKES 2 SERVINGS

One of our holiday favorites. Make sure to grate whole nutmeg, it tastes best when it's fresh.

¼ cup raw hazelnuts

2½ cups coconut water

1 cup fresh coconut meat

3 tablespoons coconut nectar

2 tablespoons lucuma powder

½ teaspoon grated nutmeg

In a high speed blender, blend the hazelnuts and coconut water together. Strain through a nut milk bag or cheesecloth to remove the hazelnut pulp. Return the mixture to the blender, add the remaining ingredients, and blend until smooth. Serve chilled.

RAWVOLUTIONARY HERO

Paul C. Bragg was an American nutritionist who advocated using deep breathing, water fasts, organic foods, distilled water, juicing, exercise, and listening to one's body as methods of prolonging life. He is the inventor of Bragg's Liquid Aminos and his health food stores, natural foods restaurants, and health spas were among the first in the United States. Bragg authored many health books including 1930's *Live Food Cook Book and Menus*.

Original Green Juice

MAKES 3 OR 4 SERVINGS

Cucumber, parsley, celery, and ginger make this juice drink perfect for nearly anyone.

3½ cucumbers

3 bunches curly parsley

1½ bunches celery

1¾-inch piece peeled fresh ginger

¼ cup fresh lemon juice

Pinch of sea salt (optional)

Juice the cucumbers, parsley, celery, and ginger using a juicer. Juice the lemon by hand or using a citrus juicer and add to the green juice. Stir in the sea salt, if using, and serve.

RAWVOLUTIONARY HERO

Hermann Sexauer was a German *Naturmensch* and raw foods advocate who emigrated to the United States in 1906. Sexauer founded Santa Barbara's first health foods store in 1934. He is quoted as having said, "Carob (pod) is excellent, because it does not ferment in the stomach," and "Olives (dried) are among the best things you can eat. They are bitter, but that aids the liver."

Save-the-World Super Veggie Tonic

MAKES 1 SERVING

Juicing is really one of the best things you can do for your health. We like putting a little of everything in just to cover all our bases.

3 tomatoes

1 carrot, peeled

½ cucumber, peeled

¼ apple

¼ lemon, peeled

½ small beet

5 leaves cabbage

3 leaves kale

10 stems dandelion greens

10 stems parsley

10 stems cilantro

2 tablespoons (12 leaves) spinach leaves

1-inch piece peeled fresh ginger

½-inch piece fresh horseradish root

1 clove garlic, peeled

Pinch of sea salt

Juice all of the ingredients except the sea salt into a large container. Stir in the sea salt and serve.

RAWVOLUTIONARY HERO

Norman Walker was among the first to advocate the drinking of fresh, raw vegetable and fruit juices, and did so until his death at 99 years of age. His Norwalk Hydraulic Press Juicer continues to be sold today. Walker considered cooked food dead and therefore, unhealthful, saying, "While such food can, and does, sustain life, it does so at the expense of progressively degenerating health, energy, and vitality."

Strawberry Sangria

.... 1

MAKES 4 OR 5 SERVINGS

A great summer drink featuring kombucha and fresh strawberries. Make a pitcher for a picnic or an evening party.

FOR THE STRAWBERRY MARINADE

- 1 pint strawberries, sliced
- 2 lemons, sliced with rind intact
- ¼ cup coconut nectar

FOR THE LEMONADE

- 1 cup fresh lemon juice
- ½ cup coconut nectar
- 6½ cups pure water
- 8 cups GT's citrus kombucha, chilled

To make the marinade, mix the ingredients in a small bowl and marinate in the refrigerator for 2 hours.

To make the lemonade, stir the ingredients together in a pitcher. Place the marinated fruit and some ice in a glass and add equal parts lemonade and your favorite flavor of kombucha.

RAWVOLUTIONARY HERO

Lawrence Armstrong was a prominent Australian nutritionist who ran the Armstrong Health Institute in the 1930s. He authored many booklets on health, including *The Life Force: Food Science as the Key to Perfect Health* (1936) and *Life Force Recipes* (1937). Armstrong once wrote: "For imparting vitality and building up resistance to diseases, raw juices have no equal and should be a part of the daily diet of young and old alike."

Sweet Black Magic Iced Coffee

1 B

MAKES 2 SERVINGS

This iced coffee is simple and delicious on a hot summer day. It's named after a song from the album *Gold* by Ryan Adams, one of our favorite musicians.

- **2 cups ice cubes**
- **2 cups Herbal Iced Coffee Concentrate (page 28)**
- **1 cup nut milk (see Almond Milk, page 24)**

Fill 2 glasses with ice and pour half of the coffee concentrate and half of the nut milk into each. Serve immediately.

RAWVOLUTIONARY HERO

Paul M. Koonin, a Russian émigré, ran a clinic called Hygeia where patients received raw, vegetarian meals. Dr. Koonin published in 1941 the book *Health Cocktails from Fruit and Vegetable Juices*. On the cover he stated: "Doctors agree that raw vegetables are the richest source of valuable mineral salts and health-giving vitamins necessary for building and maintaining good health."

Tepache

1

MAKES 4 SERVINGS

We learned about this traditional fermented Mexican brew from Abel Garcia, who has worked in the kitchen at ELR for over five years. *Gracias,* Abel!

1 medium-size pineapple

12 cups pure water

2¾ cups coconut nectar

1 tablespoon ground cinnamon

3 whole cloves

Thoroughly wash the pineapple. Remove the stem and cut the pineapple into big pieces while leaving the rind attached. Place the pieces of pineapple in a large glass jar and add 8 cups of the water, the coconut nectar, cinnamon, and cloves. Cover and let sit, unrefrigerated, for 48 hours. Strain the tepache and combine with the remaining 4 cups of water. Serve cold over ice cubes.

RAWVOLUTIONARY HERO

Francis M. Pottenger, Jr., was an American Doctor of Medicine who conducted studies involving approximately 900 cats between 1932 and 1942. Several generations of cats were divided into two groups and fed a diet of all-raw or mostly cooked foods. The cats that were fed the all-raw diet were healthy, while the cats that received the cooked meat developed various health problems and died out totally by the fourth generation.

Virgin Mimosas

MAKES 3 SERVINGS

Easy to make and refreshing, this kombucha blend is the perfect mocktail. Janabai and I still argue about who came up with the recipe.

1½ cups fresh orange juice   **3 cups GT's citrus kombucha, chilled**

Pour ½ cup of the orange juice into 3 glasses, then add 1 cup of the kombucha to each. Serve immediately.

RAWVOLUTIONARY HERO

Edward Howell was an American Doctor of Medicine and is often called the father of food enzymes. He took more than 20 years to complete his book, *Enzyme Nutrition,* where he wrote: "Humans eating an enzyme-less diet use up a tremendous amount of their enzyme potential in lavish secretions of the pancreas and other digestive organs. The result is a shortened lifespan, illness, and lower resistance to stress of all types, psychological and environmental."

Wake Up Kiss

1 **B**

MAKES 1 SERVING

Janabai's magic morning wake up drink, featuring all her faves: yerba mate tea, Teeccino hazelnut herbal coffee, reishi mushroom, and raw cacao. Relaxing and stimulating at the same time.

1 yerba mate tea bag

1 Teeccino hazelnut herbal coffee bag

1 cup hot water

½ cup nut milk (see Almond Milk, page 24)

1 tablespoon coconut nectar

1 teaspoon cacao powder

¼ teaspoon vanilla bean powder

¼ teaspoon ground cinnamon

¼ teaspoon reishi mushroom powder

In a large glass, steep both bags in the hot water. While the tea steeps, blend the nut milk, coconut nectar, cacao, vanilla powder, cinnamon, and reishi powder. Add the blended mixture to the hot tea. Serve immediately.

RAWVOLUTIONARY HERO

Artturi Virtanen, a Finnish chemist and recipient of the 1945 Nobel Prize in Chemistry, was often quoted as supporting a living foods diet. He showed that enzymes in uncooked foods are released in the chewing process. These enzymes, he posited, interact with enzymes produced by the body itself, resulting in efficient digestion.

Witches' Brew

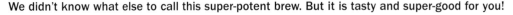

MAKES 1 SERVING

We didn't know what else to call this super-potent brew. But it is tasty and super-good for you!

- 6 carrots
- ½ apple
- 10 stems parsley
- 2 tablespoons (12 leaves) spinach leaves

- ½-inch piece fresh horseradish root
- ½-inch piece fresh ginger, peeled
- 1 clove garlic, peeled

Juice all of the ingredients into a large container. Stir and serve.

RAWVOLUTIONARY HERO

Max Gerson was a German physician who developed an alternative dietary therapy which he claimed could cure cancer and most chronic, degenerative diseases. Gerson described his approach in his book, *A Cancer Therapy: Results of 50 Cases.* His healing approach emphasized a diet of raw vegetarian food including organic juices, of which he recommended 13 glasses each day. His most famous patient was Dr. Albert Schweitzer, who claimed he was cured of his diabetes using the Gerson Therapy. Schweitzer called Gerson "a medical genius who walked among us." In 1946, Gerson was summoned to testify about his cancer therapy before a Congressional Subcommittee hearing to appropriate $100 million for a cancer research center. Gerson presented five terminal cancer patients who testified to recovering from the incurable disease, but astonishingly the bill died in the Senate. The Gerson Therapy method is illegal in the United States but is still used successfully throughout the world in clinics where it is legal.

Soups

To the uninitiated, the concept of soups that are not served piping hot may seem strange, but raw soups are full of flavor and are a great way to get a lot of condensed nutrition quickly and easily. In raw cuisine, soups are typically made in a blender, and while they are not served hot, they need not be served cold, either. A room-temperature or gently warmed raw soup can be eaten as a light meal on its own, or to whet the palate for a more decadent raw meal to come. Janabai once ate raw soups almost exclusively for three months straight! Our Superfood Soup (see page 110) is quite possibly the most popular recipe ever served at our cafés.

A Night in Tunisia Spicy Sesame Soup

1 **B**

MAKES 2 OR 3 SERVINGS

This creamy and spicy soup is filled with cilantro, purple cabbage, and coconut meat and is inspired by Janabai's favorite jazz song, written by Dizzy Gillespie. That's what the soup reminded her of when she first tasted it.

FOR THE SOUP BASE

- 1 cup pure water
- 1 cup brown sesame seeds
- ¼ cup fresh lemon juice
- 2 teaspoons chili powder
- 1½ teaspoons sea salt
- ½ teaspoon ground cumin
- ½ teaspoon ground cayenne

FOR THE SOUP ADD-INS

- ½ cup fresh coconut meat, cut into noodle-size strips
- ½ cup shredded purple cabbage
- ¼ cup chopped stemmed cilantro, plus extra for garnishing
- ¼ cup thinly sliced red onion, plus extra for garnishing

To make the soup base, combine all of the ingredients in a high speed blender, and blend until smooth.

Stir in the add-ins and serve, garnishing with additional cilantro and red onion.

RAWVOLUTIONARY HEROES

The **Nature Boys** of Southern California were philosophical descendants of the *Naturmensch* who frequented Tahquitz Canyon and Topanga Canyon in the 1930s and 1940s. The Nature Boys, who included Maximilian Sikinger, eden ahbez, Gypsy Boots, Bob Wallace, Emile Zimmerman, Buddy Rose, Gypsy Jean, and Fred Bushnoff, espoused hippie philosophies decades before the hippies of the 1960s. They lived naked outdoors, slept in trees, and ate raw, organic, and wild foods. Jack Kerouac made mention of the Nature Boys in his classic novel *On the Road*.

Carrot and Red Pepper Bisque

1 J B

MAKES 2 SERVINGS

We developed this sensual soup for a Valentine's Dinner at the café. Creamy, tangy, and savory, it makes for a delicious first course.

2 cups chopped cauliflower

1½ cups fresh coconut meat

1 cup carrot juice (requires 1 to 2 large carrots)

¼ red bell pepper

¼ cup fresh lemon juice

2 teaspoons sea salt

2 teaspoons crushed red chile peppers

3 cloves garlic, peeled

In a high speed blender, combine all of the ingredients and blend until smooth.

RAWVOLUTIONARY HERO

William Esser, an American Doctor of Naturopathic Medicine, was instrumental in promoting the concepts of Natural Hygiene and was involved in the founding of the National Health Association. He was best known for Esser's Health Ranch, a health sanitarium in Florida that specialized in plant-based nutrition and therapeutic fasting. He directed Esser's Ranch for 65 years before retiring at the age of 90.

Gazpacho

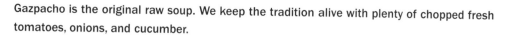

MAKES 5 OR 6 SERVINGS

Gazpacho is the original raw soup. We keep the tradition alive with plenty of chopped fresh tomatoes, onions, and cucumber.

FOR THE SOUP BASE

2 tomatoes, quartered

1 cup coconut water

⅔ cup pure water

4 teaspoons diced sun dried tomatoes

4 teaspoons fresh lemon juice

4 teaspoons olive oil

4 teaspoons apple cider vinegar

4 teaspoons coconut aminos

1 clove garlic, peeled

1 tablespoon chili powder

⅓ teaspoon sea salt

Pinch of cayenne powder

Pinch of dried oregano

FOR THE SOUP ADD-INS

⅔ cup chopped stemmed cilantro

1 tomato, chopped

⅔ cup chopped cucumber

½ cup sliced green onions

2½ tablespoons chopped yellow onion

To make the soup base, combine all of the ingredients in a high speed blender, and blend until smooth.

Stir in the add-ins and serve.

RAWVOLUTIONARY HERO

Hans Anderson, a chef, dietician, proponent of natural foods, and author, wrote in his 1944 book, *The New Food Therapy*, "From such raw materials we receive Live Food minerals and vitamins unchanged by heating. Live vegetable juices, similar to those extracted from fresh fruits, require no work on the part of digestion, but are absorbed directly into the blood and utilized by the weakest stomach."

Cream of Asparagus Soup

MAKES 2 SERVINGS

These creamy raw bisques are simple to make and taste fresh and light.

2 cups asparagus juice (requires 3 to 4 bunches of asparagus)

1 cup cashew milk (see Almond Milk, page 24)

1 clove garlic, peeled

2 tablespoons fresh lemon juice

½ teaspoon sea salt

Asparagus tips, for garnish

In a high speed blender, combine all of the ingredients and blend until smooth. Garnish with the asparagus tips.

Cream of Carrot Soup

MAKES 2 SERVINGS

2 cups nut milk (see Almond Milk, page 24)

2 cups carrot juice (requires 3 to 4 large carrots)

¼ cup fresh lemon juice

2 cloves garlic, peeled

2 teaspoons sea salt

Shredded carrot, for garnish

In a high speed blender, combine all of the ingredients and blend until smooth. Garnish with the shredded carrot.

RAWVOLUTIONARY HERO

Maximilian Sikinger published a booklet in 1946 on live foods, meditation, and sunshine called *Classical Nutrition* while living in the Santa Monica Mountains in Southern California. Sikinger frequented John and Vera Richter's Eutropheon restaurant and was particularly close friends with Nature Boy Gypsy Boots.

Red Hot Chili Soup

1 **B**

MAKES 3 OR 4 SERVINGS

This warm soup, great on a chilly day, is named for the great band the Red Hot Chili Peppers. One afternoon the front door at ELR was broken and wouldn't open, and we had to ask customers to climb through the window. One of those good sports was Anthony Kiedis of the Chili Peppers!

1½ cups chopped tomatoes	2 tablespoons olive oil
1 cup chopped peeled zucchini	4½ teaspoons chili powder
1 cup chopped cucumber	1½ teaspoons sea salt
½ cup chopped celery	1 teaspoon ground cumin
¼ cup dulse flakes	¼ teaspoon ground cayenne
¼ cup fresh lemon juice	Hot pure water
3 cloves garlic, peeled	Pumpkin seed oil, for garnish

In a high speed blender, combine all of the ingredients and blend until smooth.

This soup is meant to be served warm. When ready to serve, fill each soup bowl halfway with soup and then top off the bowl with hot water. Stir to ensure the soup and hot water are well mixed.

Garnish with a drizzle of pumpkin seed oil.

RAWVOLUTIONARY HERO

eden ahbez was a quintessential "Nature Boy" who wore robes and sandals, a beard, and long hair and walked across the United States four times. Born George Alexander Aberle, he adopted the name "eden ahbez," choosing to spell it with lower-case letters in his belief that only the words "God" and "Infinity" were worthy of capitalization. He was known to friends simply as ahbe. ahbez arrived in Los Angeles in 1941 and began playing piano in John and Vera Richter's raw food restaurant, Eutropheon, and often wrote songs and shopped them around Los Angeles. He wrote the song "Nature Boy," which was a number one hit for Nat King Cole for eight weeks in 1948, and has since become a standard. When Cole's management sought to track down the song's composer, ahbez was discovered living under an "L" in the Hollywood sign. He quickly became the focus of a media frenzy following the song's success. ahbez was then featured simultaneously in *Life*, *Time*, and *Newsweek* magazines. Frank Sinatra and Sarah Vaughan later released versions of the song, along with many others. ahbez continued to supply Cole with songs and had other compositions recorded by Sam Cooke, Eartha Kitt, and others. ahbez died in 1995 of injuries sustained in a car accident at the age of 86.

Sprouted Black Bean Chili

2 B

MAKES 3 OR 4 SERVINGS

This award-winning chili is hearty and mouthwatering, so even diehard chili fans will have a new favorite. We won the 27th Annual Topanga Chili Cook Off in the raw category with this chili. The Chili Cook Off is part of the Topanga Swap Meet and is not to be missed if you're in the area. You can sample traditional, vegetarian, and raw chili, buy or trade for cool vintage knickknacks and clothes, and hear great local L.A. bands.

FOR THE SOUP BASE

⅔ cup pure water

1½ cups chopped tomatoes

¼ cup diced sun dried tomatoes

2 tablespoons olive oil

2 teaspoons chili powder

¼ teaspoon sea salt

FOR THE ADD-INS

1½ cups chopped tomatoes

1½ cups diced celery

1½ cups crumbled Burger Patties
   (page 26)

1 cup sprouted black beans

½ cup chopped stemmed parsley

2 tablespoons diced red onion

2 tablespoons diced seeded jalapeño

To make the soup base, combine all of the ingredients in a high speed blender and blend until smooth.

Stir in the add-ins and serve.

RAWVOLUTIONARY HERO

Gypsy Boots helped bring an awareness of alternative lifestyles such as yoga and health food to mainstream America by way of wacky antics and his lovable and charming personality. Born Robert Bootzin in 1914, he dropped out of high school and spent a large part of the 1930s and '40s, wandering California with a group of self-styled vagabonds. They foraged for figs and berries, slept in caves and trees, and bathed in waterfalls. Decades ahead of the hippie movement, the group became known as the Nature Boys. Boots owned an early health food store patronized by Hollywood celebrities in the early 1960s, and even produced an all-natural, sugar-free Boots Bar. His books, *Bare Feet* and *Good Things to Eat* and the memoir *The Gypsy in Me,* gained him a cult following. On several occasions, Boots appeared on the *Steve Allen Show,* where he would often play up his role as a health advocate by swinging from a vine on stage as a Nature Boy and persuading Steve to drink one of his fruit-based health drinks, or "smoothies," as he called them. Whether cameras were rolling or not, he often liked to demonstrate his good health and vigor by throwing a football farther than many men half his age. Boots died in 2004, just days before his 90th birthday.

Superfood Soup

MAKES 1 OR 2 SERVINGS

This is the most popular dish at our café. It features Dr. Schulze's SuperFood Plus Powder, nori, avocado, cucumber, cilantro, and turmeric. It was originally an improvised creation from a staff member. Over the years it has been adapted and now has become a communal creation that the whole ELR community enjoys.

FOR THE SOUP

1½ cups coconut water

1½ cups cucumber juice (requires 1 to 2 large cucumbers)

¼ cup watercress juice

2 tablespoons fresh lemon juice

2 tablespoons flax oil

2 tablespoons Dr. Schulze's SuperFood Plus powder

1½ tablespoons olive oil

1½ tablespoons coconut aminos

½-inch piece peeled fresh ginger

2 cloves garlic, peeled

1 teaspoon curry powder

½ teaspoon sea salt

Pinch of cayenne

Pinch of turmeric

FOR THE GARNISHES

Cucumber, peeled and chopped

Cilantro, stemmed

Avocado, cubed

Nori, torn into strips

To make the soup, in a high speed blender, combine all of the ingredients and blend until smooth.

Add the garnishes in the quantities that you prefer and serve.

RAWVOLUTIONARY HERO

Bernard Jensen was an American Doctor of Chiropractic who was versed in a wide variety of holistic health care disciplines. Dr. Jensen operated health sanitariums in California for over 40 years and, in his nearly 93 years of life, wrote and published over 40 books. He once wrote: "As I see it, fresh, raw, natural foods are more compatible to our bodies than anything else."

Warm Miso Soup

MAKES 2 SERVINGS

We use adzuki bean miso in this traditional fermented favorite as well as our homemade Nofu and hemp seeds.

FOR THE SOUP

2 heaping tablespoons adzuki bean miso

3 cups pure hot water

Pinch of sea salt

FOR THE GARNISHES (OPTIONAL)

Cubed Nofu (page 29)

Nori, torn into strips

Hemp seeds

Cayenne

Turmeric

To make the soup, divide the miso between 2 soup bowls and stir into each ½ cup of hot water and a pinch of sea salt until dissolved. Add the remaining hot water equally to each bowl and stir again.

Add the optional garnishes to each bowl in the quantities that you prefer, and serve.

No, **miso** is not raw, but it is fermented, so the cultures of friendly probiotics growing in it are living. The beans themselves are in an easily digestible state as the living culture is breaking it down. Miso is an easy-to-assimilate fermented food that tastes great!

RAWVOLUTIONARY HERO

Kristine Nolfi was a Danish physician who claimed to have cured her breast cancer with "a 100 percent raw vegetable and fruit diet." Nolfi's *Raw Food Treatment of Cancer* (circa 1955) details her experience. Nolfi also stated: "Before I realized the actual importance of raw vegetable food, my attitude was exactly the same as that of other physicians—to treat the symptoms of the disease without thinking of preventing it."

Year of the Dragon Wonton Soup

MAKES 2 SERVINGS

Creamy wontons (page 118) in a spicy broth make this a delicious favorite. The lucky Year of the Dragon holds special significance for us as we were both born in that year, as were our two sons.

1½ cups pure water

1½ cups coconut water

2½ tablespoons coconut aminos

2 teaspoons fresh lemon juice

1 teaspoon olive oil

1 clove garlic, minced

Combine all of the ingredients between 2 soup bowls, and stir well, add 3 wontons each and serve.

RAWVOLUTIONARY HERO

Dugald Semple was a Scottish naturalist, a prolific author, and an advocate of simple living. In his 1956 book, *The Sunfood Way to Health,* Semple asked, "Why all this cooking when there is really no cook like old Sol?"

Appetizers

Who doesn't love appetizers? Why fill up on one thing when you can have several smaller dishes! These recipes are fun meal starters, but also great as light lunches or midday snacks!

Big Nachos

MAKES 2 SERVINGS

Heirloom blue corn chips topped with fresh guacamole and all the fixin's. A filling meal for one or great for sharing!

8 to 10 Blue Corn Chips (page 25)

2 cups Taco Meat (page 32)

1 cup Guacamole (page 28)

½ cup Salsa (page 31)

½ cup Seed Cheese (page 31)

¼ cup Mayo (page 29)

Place the corn chips on the plate, followed by the Taco Meat, Guacamole, Salsa, Seed Cheese, and Mayo.

RAWVOLUTIONARY HERO

Teresa Mitchell, a young waitress, was inspired to a fruitarian diet after reading Arnold Ehret's classic, *Rational Fasting*. Her results were so favorable that in the later part of the 1950s she wrote a moving 15-page pamphlet describing her experiences. *My Road To Health* was included in subsequent printings of Ehret's *Rational Fasting*.

Buddha-Bites Wontons

MAKES 2 OR 3 SERVINGS

Cheese-stuffed wontons wrapped in coconut curry paper.

¾ cup Cream Cheese (page 26)

1-inch piece fresh ginger, peeled and minced

¼ cup dry sea lettuce, torn into small pieces

2 Yellow Wraps (page 32)

¼ cup coconut aminos

In a small mixing bowl, combine the Cream Cheese, minced ginger, and sea lettuce and mix well.

Cut the Yellow Wraps into 2-inch squares. Put a teaspoon of the mixture in the center of each square. Squeeze the edges together and moisten with a touch of coconut aminos to seal closed. Repeat until all wonton wraps are filled.

Place each wonton on a dehydrator tray. Dehydrate at 105°F for 16 hours. Serve with coconut aminos for dipping.

RAWVOLUTIONARY HERO

Johnny Lovewisdom, an American-Finnish author who wrote over 50 books on fruitarianism, health, natural living, and spirituality, wrote: "Man was put in Paradise to live on a juicy fruit diet which produces Health, Everlasting Life and Happiness."
In the 1960s, a *Reader's Digest* article about Vilcabamba, Ecuador—an "island of immunity" from cardiovascular disease—and its abundance of fruit, led Lovewisdom to South America where he became known as the Hermit Saint of the Andes.

Cheese-Stuffed Jalapeños

2 **D** **B**

MAKES 3 OR 4 SERVINGS

Dried jalapeños are stuffed with sunflower seed cheese, perfect for dipping in cashew mayo and delicious for anyone who likes a little spiciness. Sometimes we call this dish Jalapeño Roulette because the spiciness of the peppers varies from mild to third-degree burns on your tongue. Mother Nature likes variety!

9 jalapeños, halved and seeded

1¾ cups Seed Cheese (page 31)

¾ cup flaxseeds, ground in a high speed blender

½ cup Mayo (page 29)

Using a small knife or spatula, fill each jalapeño half with Seed Cheese. Dust the cheese generously with the ground flaxseeds. Place the peppers on a dehydrator tray and dehydrate at 105°F for 12 to 24 hours, depending on whether you prefer them slightly soft or completely crunchy.

Serve with the Mayo as a dipping sauce.

RAWVOLUTIONARY HERO

H. E. Kirschner, M.D., used his "green drinks" and other vegetable juices to treat his patients. In his 1961 book, *Live Food Juices: For Vim, Vigor, Vitality,* he recounts his successes in the treatment of everything from obesity, hemorrhoids, and failing eyesight to cancer, leukemia, and kidney disease. Kirschner wrote: "There is absolutely no substitute for greens in the diet! If you refuse to eat these 'sunlight energy' foods you are depriving yourself, to a large degree, of the very essence of Life."

Cucumber Summer Rolls

1 B

MAKES 2 SERVINGS

Light and creamy rolls stuffed with cream cheese and orange wedges.

1 large cucumber, peeled

¾ cup Cream Cheese (page 26)

1 peeled orange, cut into wedges

½ cup paprika sauce (see Taquitos with Paprika Sauce, page 135)

Slice the peeled cucumbers lengthwise into paper thin slices using a mandolin or sharp knife. Roll up a slice. While holding the roll closed, spoon a tablespoon of Cream Cheese inside and stuff in a wedge of orange. Place the roll, open edge down, on a serving plate. Repeat the roll making process until all rolls have been made. Drizzle with the paprika sauce and serve.

VARIATION: Substitute other tart, sweet fruits like mango or strawberry for the orange.

RAWVOLUTIONARY HERO

Hilton Hotema was an American alternative health writer, esoteric author, and mystic. In 1962, his inspired *Man's Higher Consciousness* was published. In it, he wrote, "In the fruits and green uncooked vegetables you have food exactly as Nature has prepared it, and there is positively nothing of any sort that can equal these foods for health."

Focaccia Bread

MAKES 10 SMALL LOAVES

These delightful doughy rolls have changed the way we look at raw breads for the better. Using almond pulp, zucchini, and flax seasoned with black olives and sun dried tomatoes, this recipe was developed before ELR was even a twinkle in our eyes for a series of elegant dinners in our home called Night on Earth.

2 cups flaxseeds, ground in a high speed blender

1 cup almond pulp (see Almond Milk, page 24)

1 cup shredded peeled zucchini

¼ cup chopped raw black olives

¼ cup chopped sun dried tomatoes

¼ cup dried rosemary

2 tablespoons olive oil

1 teaspoon sea salt

In a large mixing bowl, combine all of the ingredients. Knead the mixture by hand until a consistent, doughy texture is achieved. Shape the dough into 10 small loaves. If the dough becomes tacky, use a little pure water or olive oil to smooth it out. Use a small knife to score the top of each loaf to create a baked look. Place the rolls on a mesh dehydrator sheet and dehydrate at 105°F for 24 hours.

SERVING SUGGESTIONS: These loaves are delicious when sliced and served with Pesto (page 30) or just dipped in olive oil.

RAWVOLUTIONARY HERO

Arshavir Ter Hovannessian, an Armenian living in Iran, wrote the passionate and influential *Raw Eating: or A New World Free from Diseases, Vices and Poisons* in the 1960s. In *Raw Eating*, Hovannessian wrote: "Raw vegetable food should be the only nourishment taken by man."

Everyday Flax Crackers

MAKES 27 CRACKERS

These flax crackers are terrific to eat with just about anything!

⅓ cup fresh lemon juice

¼ cup coconut aminos

½ teaspoon ground cayenne

1 tablespoon sea salt

3 cups pure water

5 cups whole flaxseeds

1 cup cilantro, stemmed and chopped

1 cup chopped tomatoes

¼ cup olive oil

In a blender, combine the lemon juice, coconut aminos, cayenne, and sea salt, and blend until smooth. Combine this mixture with the water in a large mixing bowl. Stir in the flax-seeds and let soak for 1 hour, until the liquid is absorbed.

Stir in the cilantro, tomatoes, and olive oil. Spread the mixture onto 3 dehydrator trays lined with Teflex sheets, 2 or 3 seeds thick. Score the crackers while still wet with a small knife to make 9 pieces from each tray by making 2 vertical cuts and 2 horizontal cuts. Dehydrate at 105°F for 12 hours. Flip the crackers onto a second dehydrator tray, peel off the Teflex sheets, and dehydrate for an additional 12 to 14 hours.

RAWVOLUTIONARY HEROES

George and Doris Fathman found renewed health following the teachings of Arnold Ehret and adopting a fruitarian diet. In their 1967 book *Live Foods: Natures Perfect System of Human Nutrition*, the Fathmans shared their journey to wellness, offered advice to the health seeker about the revitalizing power of a raw vegetarian diet, and presented nearly 200 live food creations.

Mock Salmon Pâté

MAKES 3 SERVINGS

This savory spread is made with walnuts, carrots, and dulse.

- 1 cup raw walnuts, well ground
- 1 tablespoon fresh lemon juice
- 1 cup roughly chopped carrots
- 1 tablespoon chopped fresh dill (stems are okay)

- ¼ cup coconut aminos
- 2 tablespoons minced yellow onion
- 2 tablespoons dulse flakes
- 1 tablespoon olive oil

In a food processor, combine all of the ingredients and process until uniform.

SERVING SUGGESTIONS: Use as a spread for Rosemary Crackers (page 131) or roll with nori to make your own mock salmon sushi.

RAWVOLUTIONARY HERO

Ann Wigmore is known as the mother of living foods, as she was an early pioneer in the use of wheatgrass juice and living foods for detoxifying and healing. Wigmore cofounded, with Viktoras Kulvinskas, the Hippocrates Health Institute in Boston in 1968 and authored several books on living foods. She wrote, "When we eat living foods, we get the maximum amount of vitamins, minerals, enzymes and other important nutrients in these foods, just as nature intended."

Pesto Bruschetta

MAKES 4 TO 6 SERVINGS

This starter combines two perfect recipes to create a classic dish.

10 Rosemary Crackers (page 131)   ¼ cup diced seeded tomatoes

1½ cups Pesto (page 30)   A few leaves of fresh basil

Top each cracker with 2 tablespoons of Pesto. Garnish each cracker with the diced tomatoes and basil.

Pesto Tomato Sliders

MAKES 2 OR 3 SERVINGS

Fresh basil blended with walnuts and olive oil, then spread on heirloom tomato slices.

2 large tomatoes (preferably heirloom)

1½ cups Pesto (page 30)

Sea salt

Slice the tomatoes into thick slices. Top each slice with a tablespoon of Pesto, sprinkle a dash of sea salt on each, and serve.

Red Pepper Hummus

MAKES 2 OR 3 SERVINGS

This creamy hummus is chickpea-free and made from sesame seeds and zucchini.

2 cups chopped peeled zucchini

1½ cups chopped red bell pepper

¾ cup raw tahini

½ cup fresh lemon juice

¼ cup olive oil

4 cloves garlic, peeled

2½ teaspoons sea salt

1½ teaspoons ground cumin

In a high speed blender, combine all of the ingredients and blend until smooth.

RAWVOLUTIONARY HERO

Viktoras Kulvinskas was born in Lithuania during World War II and eventually emigrated to the United States. Kulvinskas co-founded, with Ann Wigmore, the Hippocrates Health Institute in Boston in 1968. In 1975, he published *Survival into the 21st Century: Planetary Healers Manual.* It was an incredibly influential book in the raw food movement as it was the first to integrate environmental stewardship, activism, and self-sufficiency with the principles of raw foods.

Rosemary Crackers

MAKES 48 CRACKERS

Made with almond fiber and savory spices, these crackers are a terrific accompaniment to spreads and dips. Rosemary was once an ingredient, but the original recipe disappeared years ago (it happens)! The name stuck.

1 cup fresh lemon juice

1 cup pure water

5 cloves garlic, peeled

3 tablespoons dried sage

2 tablespoons dried thyme

2 tablespoons dried oregano

4 teaspoons sea salt

1⅔ cups almond pulp (see Almond Milk, page 24)

1⅔ cups flaxseeds, ground in a high speed blender

1⅓ cups olive oil

In a high speed blender, blend the lemon juice, pure water, garlic, sage, thyme, oregano, and salt and thoroughly blend. Transfer to a mixing bowl and add the almond pulp, flaxseeds, and olive oil.

Knead the mixture by hand until a consistent, doughy texture is achieved. Spread the mixture onto 2 dehydrator trays lined with Teflex sheets (add a little extra water if the mixture is too thick to spread evenly). Score the crackers before dehydrating, dividing each tray into 24 crackers by scoring 3 cuts vertically and 5 cuts horizontally. Dehydrate for 12 to 14 hours at 105°F. Flip the crackers onto another dehydrator tray, peel off the Teflex sheets, and dehydrate for an additional 12 to 14 hours. Store in a cool, dry place until ready to serve.

RAWVOLUTIONARY HERO

Morris Krok, a South African who migrated to California, sought solutions to his own health problems and was influenced by natural healing writers Louis Kuhne, Arnold Ehret, Dugald Semple, Essie Honiball, and Johnny Lovewisdom. In the article *A Yogic Perspective,* Krok stated "to heal and avoid illness, one must alkalinize the body through a diet of predominately raw fruits and vegetables."

Sea Cakes with Cilantro Chutney

③ P B D

MAKES 6 TO 8 SERVINGS

These croquettes are stuffed with sea lettuce and veggies and topped with a zingy cilantro chutney, mayo, and spicy horseradish. This recipe was inspired by a dish at the vegan restaurant that I love—Real Food Daily.—*Janabai*

FOR THE SEA CAKES

2 cups shredded carrots

¾ cup dry sea lettuce

¾ cup chopped celery

¾ cup almond pulp (see Almond Milk, page 24)

½ cup chopped fresh dill

⅓ cup chopped green onions

⅓ cup dulse flakes

⅓ cup olive oil

¼ cup fresh lemon juice

1 teaspoon sea salt

4 cloves garlic, peeled

5 tablespoons flaxseeds, ground in a high speed blender

FOR THE CILANTRO CHUTNEY

1 cup stemmed cilantro

½ cup chopped green onions

¼ cup fresh lemon juice

1½ tablespoons olive oil

1 jalapeño, seeded and chopped

2 cloves garlic, peeled

1 teaspoon sea salt

¼ teaspoon ground cumin

½ cup Mayo (page 29)

Shredded horseradish root, for garnish

Dried arame, for garnish

To make the sea cakes, combine all of the ingredients except the ground flaxseeds in a food processor and process well.

Scoop out ½ cup of the mixture and roll into a ball. Flatten the ball into a patty. Dip each side of the patty into the ground flaxseeds. Repeat this procedure for each patty. Gently place the patties on a Teflex-lined dehydrator tray and dehydrate for 12 to 14 hours at 105°F. Refrigerate the patties until ready to serve.

To make the chutney, in a food processor, combine all of the ingredients and process well.

When ready to serve, top each sea cake with 1 tablespoon of the chutney and a dollop of Mayo. Garnish the top of each sea cake with fresh, shredded horseradish and dried arame.

RAWVOLUTIONARY HERO

John H. Tobe, born circa 1906, was a world traveler, researcher, naturalist, nurseryman, farmer, publisher, and author. In his 1969 book, *John H. Tobe's Health Giving, Life Saving No-Cook Book,* he writes: "I also endorse the eating of as much uncooked food as possible because I have learned that only through the medium of uncooked foods, do true health and well-being lie."

Taquitos with Paprika Sauce

③ B P D

MAKES 3 OR 4 SERVINGS

Crispy coconut rolls stuffed with walnut Taco Meat and drizzled with a sweet and spicy sauce.

FOR THE TAQUITOS

2 Yellow Wraps (page 32)

1½ cups Taco Meat (page 32)

Olive oil

FOR THE PAPRIKA SAUCE

¾ cup olive oil

¼ cup apple cider vinegar

6 tablespoons coconut nectar

1½ tablespoons paprika

1 teaspoon sea salt

2 cloves garlic, peeled

To make the Taquitos, cut each wrap into four 3 by 4-inch rectangles. Layer 3 tablespoons of the Taco Meat across one edge of a wrap. Roll the wrap closed and moisten the edges with a small amount of olive oil to seal the roll. Repeat to make 8 Taquitos. Place the Taquitos on a dehydrator tray. Dehydrate for 12 to 14 hours at 105°F.

To make the sauce, in a high speed blender, combine all of the ingredients and blend until smooth. Refrigerate until ready to serve.

To serve, place the Taquitos on a serving plate and drizzle with the paprika sauce.

SERVING SUGGESTION: Serve with an additional dipping sauce such as Mayo (page 29).

RAWVOLUTIONARY HERO

Father Yod (pronounced *Yode*) founded a spiritual commune in 1970s Los Angeles known as the Source Family, whose 140 members lived together in a rented Hollywood Hills mansion called the Mother House. They practiced meditation, chanting, breathwork, and raw vegetarianism. Yod was also the lead singer in the family's psychedelic rock band, Ya Ho Wha 13, and owned a very successful restaurant on Hollywood's Sunset Strip called The Source. Serving local, organic, vegetarian, and raw foods, The Source was frequented by John Lennon, Marlon Brando, and Warren Beatty. It remained in business from 1969 until the late 1990s, and was featured in Woody Allen's film *Annie Hall*.

RAWVOLUTIONARY HERO

T.C. Fry read Herbert Shelton's *Superior Nutrition* in 1970 and instantly adopted a lifestyle based on the principles of Natural Hygiene. He soon overcame many long-standing health problems and began teaching Natural Hygiene with devoted fervor. In the 1980s, Fry's *Healthful Living* magazine reached an estimated 30,000 subscribers. Fry once wrote: "Throughout my writings and lessons, I have cited ample scientific literature that establishes our fruitarian disposition."

Spinach Cheese Dip

1 B

MAKES 2 OR 3 SERVINGS

A more healthful version of an American favorite.

2 cups chopped avocados

1 cup chopped spinach, briefly marinated
in 1 tablespoon olive oil

1 cup raw walnuts

¼ cup chopped fresh basil, plus more for
garnish

2 tablespoons fresh lemon juice

1 tablespoon coconut aminos

1 teaspoon nutritional yeast

½ teaspoon ground black pepper

In a high speed blender, combine all of the ingredients and blend until smooth. Refrigerate until ready to serve. Garnish with basil just before serving.

SERVING SUGGESTIONS: Serve as a dip for bell peppers, celery, and carrots, or serve with Everyday Flax Crackers (page 126).

RAWVOLUTIONARY HERO

Dick Gregory is an American comedian, social activist, social critic, writer, and entrepreneur and is ranked at number 82 on Comedy Central's list of the 100 Greatest Stand-Ups of all time. In the 1970s, Gregory, an African American, posited that slaves had eaten not soul food but "soil food," which included fresh, organic fruits and vegetables. Gregory eventually adopted a fruitarian diet as described in his 1973 book, *Dick Gregory's Natural Diet for Folks Who Eat.*

Salads & Side Dishes

Someone once asked us why we didn't serve salad at our café in Santa Monica. We thought that was funny because all raw food meals are essentially salads in different forms! Plus, we figured any restaurant can make a salad, but how many can make a raw enchilada? We realized, however, that folks love a traditional salad too! Salads were such a big part of our lives that we never really saw them as requiring recipes, but we started including more salads on the menu from that day forward.

Cactus Salad

MAKES 2 SERVINGS

Nopales cactus, tomatoes, fresh corn kernels, green onions, and cilantro in a light dressing.

FOR THE SALAD

3 cups fresh nopalitos

1 cup raw corn kernels cut from the cob

1 tomato, chopped

¼ cup sliced green onions

¼ cup chopped stemmed cilantro

FOR THE DRESSING

½ cup fresh lemon juice

½ cup olive oil

2½ teaspoons sea salt

Pinch of ground cayenne

Combine all of the salad and dressing ingredients in a mixing bowl and toss until the dressing is well distributed. Refrigerate until ready to serve.

Nopales are the edible pads of the prickly pear cactus, with the spines removed. These fleshy pads are flat and about hand-size and can be purple or green. They are particularly common in their native Mexico where the plant is eaten regularly.

RAWVOLUTIONARY HERO

Patricia Bragg has been delivering the living foods message for decades. She is a lecturer, a Doctor of Naturopathy, and the author of many health books. She calls herself the Leader of the Bragg Crusades, referring to the lifestyle tenets first promoted by her late father-in-law, Paul C. Bragg, nearly a century ago. Patricia Bragg's company produces Bragg Apple Cider Vinegar, Bragg Liquid Aminos, and other products popular in raw food circles.

RAWVOLUTIONARY HERO

Essie Honiball, born in 1924, was a South African who wrote extensively on fruitarianism, raw nutrition, fasting, and detoxification. On fruitarianism, she said: "It changed my life from dying to living." Honiball wrote several books about her experiences with the fruit diet, including *I Live On Fruit.* According to her writings, she sustained an exclusive fruitarian diet for a period of twenty years without break.

Café Salad

MAKES 2 SERVINGS

Our favorite simple salad at home is made just like this with plenty of avocados, whole-leaf dulse, tomatoes, and raw olives.

6 cups baby greens or mesclun mix

1 avocado, sliced

2 medium tomatoes, chopped

¼ cup raw black olives, chopped

¼ cup whole-leaf dulse, torn into bite-sized pieces

¾ cup Garlic Cream Dressing (page 27)

In a large salad bowl, toss the greens with the avocado, tomatoes, olives, and dulse. Mix in the Garlic Cream Dressing or serve it on the side.

RAWVOLUTIONARY HERO

Aris LaTham entered the New York City raw food scene with the opening of the Harlem-based Sunfired Foods, one of the first organic produce co-ops where he debuted his raw food recipes in 1979. In the late 1990s, Aris opened Ozone and the Sunfire Juice Club, other pioneering raw food restaurants in New York City.

Celery Caesar Salad

MAKES 2 SERVINGS

This scrumptious Caesar salad features a fresh horseradish dressing, crunchy celery, rosemary croutons, and capers.

FOR THE DRESSING

- ¼ cup olive oil
- 2 tablespoons dulse flakes
- 2 tablespoons fresh lemon juice
- 2 tablespoons coconut aminos
- 2 tablespoons chopped raw horseradish root
- Pinch of sea salt
- ½ teaspoon ground black pepper
- 2 cloves garlic, peeled
- Capers, for garnish
- Rosemary Crackers (page 131), crumbled into crouton-size bits

FOR THE SALAD

- 6 cups chopped romaine lettuce
- ½ cup chopped celery

To make the dressing, in a high speed blender, combine all of the ingredients and blend until smooth.

To make the salad, toss the dressing with the romaine lettuce and the celery. Garnish with the capers and the rosemary croutons.

RAWVOLUTIONARY HERO

Stan Glaser founded Florida's Glaser Organic Farms in 1980. The farm grows organic produce and manufactures raw, vegan packaged food products that are prepared in the farm's own kitchen and sold at farmers' markets and in health food stores nationwide. Glaser has been quoted as stating: "Raw food was the original food."

Creamed Spinach

MAKES 3 OR 4 SERVINGS

This creamy side dish whips up quickly and is a great way to get your spinach!

¼ cup fresh lemon juice

¼ cup coconut aminos

1 clove garlic, peeled

1 cup raw cashews

1 tablespoon nutritional yeast

4 cups spinach leaves

In a high speed blender, combine all of the ingredients except the spinach and blend until smooth.

Add the dressing to the spinach leaves. Allow it to marinate for 30 minutes before serving.

SERVING SUGGESTION: This creamy dressing is great served on kale as well.

RAWVOLUTIONARY HERO

Elizabeth Baker, previously a university professor, was diagnosed with Addison's Disease and colorectal cancer and claims to have reversed both conditions by adhering to a raw foods diet. Baker is the author of several natural nutrition books including 1981's *The Uncook Book.* Baker lived an energetic life, lecturing and writing until her passing at the age of 92.

Greek Salad with Cashew Feta

2 **B**

MAKES 2 SERVINGS

Fresh spinach, red onion, and our delicious cashew feta are topped with a tangy Greek dressing.

FOR THE DRESSING

¼ cup olive oil	2 teaspoons fresh lemon juice
3 tablespoons pine nuts	1 teaspoon paprika
3 tablespoons pure water	1 clove garlic, peeled
1 tablespoon apple cider vinegar	½ teaspoon sea salt

FOR THE SALAD

6 cups baby spinach leaves	Peppercorns, for garnish
¼ cup thinly sliced red onion	½ cup, cubed cashew feta (see Nofu, page 29)
2 tablespoons chopped fresh dill	

To make the dressing, in a high speed blender, combine all of the ingredients and blend until smooth.

To make the salad, toss the dressing with the spinach leaves, red onion, and dill. Garnish with the peppercorns and cashew feta.

RAWVOLUTIONARY HERO

Mark Mathew Braunstein is a photographer, lecturer, and the author of the 1981 book *Radical Vegetarianism,* in which he writes, "Eat foods as raw, as whole, and as fresh as possible."

RAWVOLUTIONARY HEROES

Jim Karas and **Carolyn Griesse** co-authored the 1981 book *The Raw Foods Diet: The Vital Gift of Enzymes.* Karas has since become a sought-after speaker and weight-loss and fitness adviser and a number one *New York Times* bestselling author.

THE RAWVOLUTION LIFESTYLE

While not strictly related to eating raw foods, the following practices complement the living foods way of life. These are by no means exhaustive or thorough descriptions, only introductions. Those who wish to learn more about any of the following topics can find countless resources on them. We have personally experienced the benefits and insights derived from all of these practices.

Activism

Activism is a form of participatory democracy and consists of efforts to raise public awareness and to promote social change. Activism offers a chance to be a voice for the voiceless whether they are people in need, animals, the environment, or any cause close to your heart.

Never doubt that a small group of thoughtful, committed citizens can change the world. Indeed, it is the only thing that ever has.

—Margaret Mead

Alternative Medicine

Alternative medicine is any practice claiming to heal that does not fall within the realm of conventional medicine. Methods may be based on traditional medicine, folk knowledge, spiritual beliefs, or newly conceived approaches to healing. Though too numerous to mention in their entirety, these practices may include acupuncture, aromatherapy, Ayurveda, chelation therapy, Chinese medicine, chiropractic, homeopathy, hydrotherapy, hypnosis, iridology, kinesiology, ozone therapy, reflexology, reiki, and rolfing.

The doctor of the future will give no medication, but will interest his patients in the care of the human frame, diet and in the cause and prevention of disease. **—Thomas Edison**

Astrology

Astrology holds that there is a relationship between astronomical phenomena and events in the human world. A central principle of astrology is integration within the cosmos, that the individual and its environment are a single organism. Skeptics of astrology can acknowledge that the moon affects ocean tides but somehow find it preposterous that the sun, moon, and planets might affect other earthly bodies.

We are born at a given moment, in a given place and, like vintage years of wine, we have the qualities of the year and of the season of which we are born. Astrology does not lay claim to anything more. —Carl Jung

Cleansing

Cleansing is a broad term used to describe the process of detoxifying the body's internal system and organs with the use of fasting, water, herbs, or other means.

To lengthen thy life, lessen thy meals. The best of all medicines is rest and fasting.

—Benjamin Franklin

Earthing/Grounding

Earthing is the simple practice of "grounding" yourself—that is, reconnecting your body to the natural electrical field in the Earth's surface—and restoring the body's innate electrical balance. This can be accomplished by simply connecting any part of the skin's surface to the earth, a tree, or a body of water or by using earthing technologies when indoors.

I strongly believe also that Earthing is not just to remedy health issues already present, but also to assist our bodies in staying healthy. I have come to think of this as about the most natural form of prevention and anti-aging medicine you can find. —Clint Ober

Environmentalism

Environmentalism is a broad philosophy, ideology, and social movement regarding concerns for environmental conservation and improvement of the health of the environment.

What's the use of a fine house if you haven't got a tolerable planet to put it on?

—Henry David Thoreau

Food Self-Sufficiency

Food self-sufficiency is the process of reducing one's dependence on the industrial food supply through the utilization of local food systems. These may include diverse solutions such as the growing of one's own food, patronizing farmers' markets, foraging, or other means.

If people let the government decide what foods they eat and what medicines they take, their bodies will soon be in as a sorry state as the souls who live under tyranny.

—Thomas Jefferson

Meditation

Meditation is any form of a family of practices in which practitioners train their minds to enter a mode of consciousness in which the mind becomes still. Herein, frantic daily thoughts are replaced with a greater sense of peace and equilibrium.

Meditation is listening to the Divine within.

—Edgar Cayce

Outdoorism

Outdoorism can, of course, encompass anything done out of doors. Whether it is hiking, swimming, climbing rocks, or simply laying in the sun, nature offers something that simply cannot be replicated indoors.

God enters by a private door into each individual.

—Ralph Waldo Emerson

Pranayama

Pranayama is a Sanskrit word meaning "extension of the life force." One of the eight limbs of yoga, Pranayama promotes proper breathing by way of exercises aimed at lengthening, expanding, and controlling the breath.

Yoga teaches us to cure what need not be endured and endure what cannot be cured.

—B. K. S. Iyengar

Spirituality

Spirituality can refer to an inner path enabling a person to discover the essence of his or her being and is often experienced as a source of inspiration or orientation in life. In a wide variety of traditions, spirituality is seen as a path toward one or more of the following: a higher state of awareness, perfection of one's own being, wisdom, finding purpose and meaning in life, or communion with God or creation.

Forget not that the earth delights to feel your bare feet and the winds long to play with your hair.

—Kahlil Gibran

Sungazing

Sungazing is a practice that involves staring at the sun, during sunrise and sunset hours, for nourishment and well-being.

If I had to choose a religion, the sun as the universal giver of life would be my god.

—Napoleon Bonaparte

Yoga

Yoga is a physical, mental, and spiritual discipline originating in ancient India. The Sanskrit word *yoga* has the literal meaning of "to yoke," meaning to join, to unite, or to attach. Yoga is the method of yoking the "lower" (egoistic) personality or passions, to the "higher" via a process of sublimation.

Yoga teaches how to still the mind through breath-control and attain higher states of awareness.

—Paramahansa Yogananda

Creamy Wakame Seaweed Salad

MAKES 2 SERVINGS

This yummy side salad is an awesome way to enjoy seaweed, and the creamy sauce makes it taste rich and hearty. We originally made this dish with a seaweed called "sea palm," but it's difficult to get these days. If you can get your hands on some, we highly recommend it as a variation!

FOR THE DRESSING

- ¼ cup olive oil
- ¼ cup raw walnuts
- 3 tablespoons fresh lemon juice
- 3 tablespoons coconut aminos
- 6 cloves garlic, peeled
- 3-inch piece peeled fresh ginger

FOR THE SALAD

- 1⅓ cups ribbed wakame, soaked for 1 hour and drained
- 1 cup chopped stemmed cilantro
- ⅔ cup whole-leaf dulse
- ⅓ cup thinly sliced green onions
- 3 tablespoons black sesame seeds

To make the dressing, in a high speed blender, combine all of the ingredients and blend until smooth.

To make the salad, combine the wakame, cilantro, dulse, green onions, and sesame seeds in a large salad bowl. Toss the salad with the dressing. Refrigerate for 30 minutes before serving.

RAWVOLUTIONARY HERO

Charles Gerras, author of the 1980s book, *Feasting on Raw Foods,* wrote: "One of the simplest and best cuisines of all has gone largely unnoticed and its core is literally and figuratively in our own garden—the fresh tasting, wonderfully nourishing, palate-tingling world of raw foods."

Kinpira

1

MAKES 2 SERVINGS

This is our take on a traditional Japanese marinated dish. We love burdock root! It has an incredible earthy sweetness that deserves more attention. Note that in 1896, Russian writer Leo Tolstoy wrote about a tiny shoot of burdock he saw in a plowed field: "black from dust but still alive and red in the center . . . It makes me want to write. It asserts life to the end, and alone in the midst of the whole field, somehow or other had asserted it."

1½ cups julienned burdock root

1 cup julienned carrot

¼ cup cold-pressed sesame oil

2 tablespoons coconut aminos

2 tablespoons apple cider vinegar

1 tablespoon black sesame seeds

1 tablespoon brown sesame seeds

Combine and toss all ingredients in a mixing bowl. Refrigerate until ready to serve.

RAWVOLUTIONARY HEROES

Harvey and Marilyn Diamond have introduced millions to vegetarianism and living foods through their numerous, extremely popular publications. In their *New York Times* bestselling book, *Fit For Life,* possibly the bestselling book on health and nutrition ever written, the Diamonds proclaim: "Any food which has been cooked at a temperature higher than 130 degrees F has been subjected to the death sentence of its enzymes and is nothing but dead food."

Not-So-Fried Rice

1

MAKES 2 SERVINGS

This zen dish features minced burdock rice and finely cut green onions in a light and tangy marinade.

3 cups finely chopped burdock root

½ cup chopped green onions

2 tablespoons coconut aminos

4 teaspoons cold-pressed sesame oil

In a small mixing bowl, mix all of the ingredients. Refrigerate until ready to serve.

RAWVOLUTIONARY HERO

Udo Erasmus was born in Poland during his parents' exodus from Latvia in World War II. He authored the health classic, *Fats That Heal, Fats That Kill,* in which he writes: "When cooked food is eaten, a defense reaction occurs in the tissues of the stomach and digestive tract. This reaction is similar to the reaction we find in infections and around tumors and involves the accumulation of white blood cells, swelling and a fever-like increase of temperature of the stomach and intestinal tissues."

Simple Kale Salad

MAKES 2 OR 3 SERVINGS

Simple, noble kale combined with a little lemon, olive oil, and Himalayan pink salt makes this zen dish a staple.

8 cups torn stemmed kale

½ teaspoon sea salt

2½ teaspoons fresh lemon juice

1½ tablespoons olive oil

Massage the kale with the sea salt. Allow it to sit for 10 minutes. Massage in the lemon juice and let sit for an additional 10 minutes. Finally, add the olive oil. Refrigerate until ready to serve.

SERVING SUGGESTIONS: Simple Kale Salad is great on its own, as the base for another salad, or as the stuffing in a great wrap.

RAWVOLUTIONARY HERO

Bill Pearl is an American former bodybuilder and four-time winner of the Mr. Universe contest. Arnold Schwarzenegger once wrote: "Bill Pearl never talked me into becoming a vegetarian, but he did convince me that a vegetarian could become a champion bodybuilder." Pearl's 1986 book, *Getting Stronger,* is widely regarded as the world's best book on general weight training and has sold hundreds of thousands of copies. In it, he writes: "Eat some raw or 'living' foods. If cooking is required, cook as little as possible to preserve enzymes and other nutrients."

Superfood Salad

1

MAKES 2 SERVINGS

This nutrient-dense salad is for kale lovers and features Dr. Schulze's Superfood powder.

4 cups Simple Kale Salad (page 155)

2 cups baby greens or mesclun mix

1 avocado, sliced

1 cup cherry tomatoes, halved

1 sheet nori, torn into bite-size pieces

2 tablespoons Dr. Schulze's SuperFood Plus powder

⅓ cup flax oil

In a large bowl, top the kale salad and the greens with the avocado, tomatoes, nori, and SuperFood powder. Toss with flax oil or serve it on the side.

RAWVOLUTIONARY HERO

George Malkmus, born in 1934, is a Christian minister who, in 1976, was diagnosed with colon cancer. Malkmus wrote: "Within a year of changing my diet to a pure, raw, vegetarian diet, not only was my tumor gone, but so were all the other physical problems I was suffering." Malkmus is the author of several books on his brand of raw food living, which he calls the Hallelujah Diet. Reverend Malkmus and his wife Rhonda founded and run Hallelujah Acres, a living foods retreat center, café, and health food store in North Carolina.

Teriyaki Seaweed Salad

 1 **B**

MAKES 2 SERVINGS

Sea lettuce is delicious—especially in a sweet and spicy yacon dressing served atop baby bok choy.

FOR THE DRESSING

- ½ cup olive oil
- ¼ cup yacon syrup
- 2 tablespoons coconut aminos
- 1 tablespoon fresh lemon juice
- 3 cloves garlic, peeled
- 1-inch piece peeled fresh ginger
- ½ teaspoon chili powder

FOR THE SALAD

- 1½ cups dry sea lettuce, torn into bite-sized pieces
- 1½ cups chopped baby bok choy
- Black and brown sesame seeds, for garnish

To make the dressing, in a high speed blender, combine all of the ingredients and blend until smooth.

To make the salad, in a mixing bowl, toss the sea lettuce and baby bok choy with the dressing until well-coated. Refrigerate until ready to serve. Garnish with a sprinkle of black and brown sesame seeds and serve.

RAWVOLUTIONARY HERO

Steve Meyerowitz was dubbed "Sproutman" in a 1979 feature article in *Vegetarian Times Magazine*, the same year that he invented the fabric sprouting bag. He has also invented home sprouting devices, and supplies his growing kits and a full line of organic sprouting seeds via mail order. Meyerowitz wrote *Sprouts: the Miracle Food*, as well as several other books on sprouting, juicing, and natural health.

Yogi's Curried Vegetables

1 B

MAKES 2 SERVINGS

A naturally sweet and creamy coconut sauce poured over cauliflower, broccoli, and zucchini. Matt invented this recipe to satisfy requests for a dish containing no garlic or onion, both of which are considered by some yogis to be too stimulating for the meditative mind. I wonder if they were referring to the breath of the garlic-eater sitting next to them while they tried to meditate!

FOR THE VEGETABLE MIX

2 cups chopped cauliflower

1½ cups chopped broccoli

1½ cups cubed peeled zucchini

1 teaspoon sea salt

FOR THE DRESSING

1⅓ cups coconut butter

⅔ cup coconut water

⅓ cup fresh lemon juice

2 tablespoons stone-ground mustard

1-inch piece peeled fresh ginger

1 tablespoon garam masala

1 teaspoon ground turmeric

1 teaspoon ground coriander

Pinch of cayenne

To prepare the vegetable mix, in a mixing bowl, combine the chopped vegetables and rub them thoroughly with the sea salt. Allow them to sit while making the dressing.

To make the dressing, in a high speed blender, combine all of the ingredients and blend until smooth.

Combine the vegetables and the dressing and mix until the veggies are well coated. Serve immediately.

RAWVOLUTIONARY HERO

Daniel Reid is the author of numerous books on Eastern philosophy and medicine and self-healing practices. In his 1989 book, *The Tao of Health, Sex, and Longevity,* he writes: "People who live on primarily cooked-food diets waste an enormous amount of energy every day digesting and eliminating stagnant piles of 'dead' food in their systems."

Taco Salad

MAKES 2 SERVINGS

We would often have Guacamole, Salsa, and Seed Cheese left over from preparing The Box meals for RAWvolution. Matt would finish them up by piling them atop a big bowl of lettuce. Taco Salad was born!

6 cups chopped romaine lettuce

1 cup Taco Meat (page 32)

1 cup Guacamole (page 28)

½ cup Salsa (page 31)

½ cup Seed Cheese (page 31)

¼ cup Mayo (page 29)

Place 3 cups of romaine lettuce on each of 2 serving plates. Equally distribute, in layers, the Taco Meat, Guacamole, Salsa, Seed Cheese, and a dollop of Mayo. Serve immediately.

RAWVOLUTIONARY HERO

Joe Alexander, a raw fooder since 1976, is a visual artist who believes his most "outstanding discovery in life is the value of raw food diet in increasing the beauty, clarity and strength of one's artwork." In his 1990 book, *Blatant Raw Foodist Propaganda!*, Alexander exclaims: "When you take up the raw food diet, you become a new and different and better person. You don't just stay the same old person, only a little healthier. The raw food diet doesn't so much 'improve you' as 'replace you' with somebody better!"

Entrées

Raw food entrées are very gratifying to create. Occasionally complex, they burst with flavors and textures that make the preparation all the more worthwhile. A well-crafted entrée is the pièce de résistance of any thoughtful meal and raw food meals are certainly no exception!

ENTRÉES

Atlantis Rolls

MAKES 2 ROLLS

Yummy sushi rolls stuffed with our mock tuna, stone-ground mustard, and raw pickles. That's right, pickles can be raw! Cold-processed pickles are not boiled prior to pickling. We use and recommend pickles brined only in pure water and sea salt.

FOR THE MAYO

⅔ cup coconut water

Generous ½ cup raw macadamia nuts, cashews, pine nuts, or a combination

1 clove garlic, peeled

1 teaspoon sea salt

2 tablespoons stone-ground mustard

FOR THE MOCK TUNA

1 cup soaked raw sunflower seeds (see Note), ground in a food processor

1½ stalks celery, diced

2 green onions, diced

4 teaspoons dried dill

2 teaspoons dulse flakes

FOR THE ROLLS

2 sheets nori

2 tablespoons stone-ground mustard

1 raw pickle, diced

To make the Mayo, in a high speed blender, combine all of the ingredients and blend until smooth.

To make the mock tuna, in a mixing bowl, combine all of the ingredients with the blended Mayo. Mix well.

To assemble the sushi rolls, lay out 1 sheet of nori on a clean, dry surface. Place half of the mock tuna in a narrow layer along the length of the sheet, about ½ inch from the edge closest to you. Spoon 1 tablespoon of mustard across the top of the tuna layer. Layer half of the diced pickle along the top, keeping all ingredients in a narrow line. Fold the edge of the nori closest to you over the filling. Gently roll the nori away from you, tightly and evenly, into a firm, snugly wrapped roll. Seal the exposed edge of the nori to the roll by wetting it with a little pure water. Repeat to make the second roll.

Cut each roll into 6 pieces with a sharp knife. Serve immediately.

NOTE: Soak the sunflower seeds in pure water for 2 to 4 hours then thoroughly drain.

RAWVOLUTIONARY HERO

Jay Kordich was diagnosed with bladder cancer over 60 years ago, which he treated by consuming 13 eight-ounce glasses of vegetable juice each day. He has since had no recurrence of cancer. In 1989, Kordich began appearing on national television as The Juiceman, promoting juicing and his own brand of juicer. Kordich authored the *New York Times* bestselling book, *The Juiceman's Power of Juicing*, in which he states: "Every day I nurture the trillions of cells in my body with fresh juices and raw foods."

Bagel Sandwiches

This bagel sandwich is always a hit. A savory black olive bagel surrounds cashew Cream Cheese, fresh tomato, onion, and basil.

FOR THE BAGELS

1 cup flaxseeds, ground in a high speed blender

½ cup almond pulp (see Almond Milk, page 24)

½ cup shredded peeled zucchini

2 tablespoons chopped raw black olives

2 tablespoons chopped fresh or dried rosemary

1 tablespoon olive oil

½ teaspoon sea salt

FOR THE SANDWICHES

¾ cup Cream Cheese (page 26)

1 medium tomato, thinly sliced

8 thin slices yellow onion

Fresh basil leaves

To make the bagels, in a large mixing bowl, combine all of the ingredients. Knead the mixture by hand until a consistent, doughy texture is achieved. Shape the dough into 4 bagels by hand (if the dough becomes tacky, use a little pure water or olive oil to smooth it out). Place the bagels on a dehydrator tray and dehydrate at 105°F for 24 hours, or until the bagels are dry on the outside and soft, but not wet, on the inside.

To assemble the sandwiches, slice a bagel in half and spread 1½ tablespoons of Cream Cheese on both halves. Place a slice of tomato on top of the Cream Cheese on each half. Put 2 thin slices of onion and a few fresh basil leaves on the bottom half of the bagel and recombine the two halves to make a sandwich. Repeat with the remaining bagels.

RAWVOLUTIONARY HERO

Brian Clement has directed the Hippocrates Health Institute in Florida since 1980, conducted countless seminars and lectures around the globe, and authored a number of books on health, spirituality, and natural healing. In his book, *Hippocrates LifeForce*, Dr. Clement writes: "Lifeforce is the inherent electrical charge from nature that regenerates human health. It is most readily accessible in raw living food."

Californication Rolls

These fun sushi rolls are filled with the foods that California hippies are known for: hemp seeds, mushrooms, and jalapeños.

FOR THE SUSHI RICE

2 cups cauliflower florets

3 tablespoons pine nuts or cashews

3 tablespoons hemp seeds

2 tablespoons olive oil

1 teaspoon sea salt

FOR THE ROLLS

4 nori sheets

½ cup sliced button mushrooms, marinated for 20 minutes in Garlic Cream Dressing to cover (page 27)

1 avocado, sliced into spears

2 tablespoons minced seeded jalapeños

1 cup Garlic Cream Dressing (page 27)

To make the rice, place all of the ingredients in a food processor and process until a consistent, rice-like texture is achieved.

To assemble the rolls, lay out 1 sheet of nori on a clean, dry surface. Place a narrow layer of sushi rice along the length of the nori sheet, about ½ inch from the edge closest to you. Spoon 2 tablespoons of the marinated mushrooms across the top of the rice layer. Layer one-fourth of the avocado spears along the top and top with one-fourth of the jalapeños, keeping all ingredients in a narrow line. Fold the edge of the nori closest to you over the filling. Gently roll the nori away from you, tightly and evenly, into a firm, snugly wrapped roll. Seal the exposed edge of the nori to the roll by wetting it with a little pure water. Repeat to make 3 more rolls.

Cut each roll into 6 pieces with a sharp knife. Serve immediately with the Garlic Cream Dressing as a dipping sauce.

VARIATION: For a crunchy, spicy roll, top each roll with Taco Meat (page 32) and Paprika Sauce (see page 135).

RAWVOLUTIONARY HEROES

Jameth and Kim Sheridan wrote the first contemporary and first *fully-vegan* raw recipe book, *Uncooking with Jameth and Kim*, in 1991. *Uncooking* included a recipe for a Flax Tortilla, which is the flax cracker we know today. Jameth Sheridan, a Doctor of Naturopathic Medicine, now conducts research on live food nutrition and produces healing programs and products through his company, HealthForce Nutritionals.

Cocophoria Sandwiches

MAKES 2 SANDWICHES

Our cocophoria meat (like a coconut jerky) is delicious, especially served with creamy Mayo, fresh tomato, onion, and lettuce atop our crispy RAWvolution's Famous Onion Bread.

FOR THE COCOPHORIA MEAT

4 cups coconut meat

5 teaspoons olive oil

5 teaspoons coconut aminos

4 teaspoons fresh lemon juice

2 teaspoons curry powder

Pinch of ground cayenne

FOR THE SANDWICHES

4 leaves romaine lettuce

4 slices RAWvolution's Famous Onion Bread (page 30)

4 thin slices yellow onion

1 small tomato, sliced

¼ cup Mayo (page 29)

To make the cocophoria meat, cut the coconut meat into thin strips, approximately 1 by 3 inches. In a mixing bowl, combine the coconut with all of the remaining ingredients and mix well. Cover and refrigerate to marinate for 2 to 4 hours. The longer it marinates, the richer the flavor will be.

Place the meat on a dehydrator tray lined with a Teflex sheet and dehydrate for 12 to 14 hours. The texture will be great for sandwiches at this point. If you prefer a drier consistency, remove the Teflex sheet and dehydrate for an additional 6 to 8 hours.

To assemble the sandwiches, place the lettuce on 2 pieces of RAWvolution's Famous Onion Bread. Layer the cocophoria meat next, topped with onion slices, tomato slices, and Mayo. Top each sandwich with a second piece of RAWvolution's Famous Onion Bread and serve.

NOTE: You may have extra cocophoria meat to enjoy on the side or to make additional sandwiches.

RAWVOLUTIONARY HERO

Don Kidson adopted a raw foods lifestyle in 1986 after the death of his wife from cancer. Kidson hosted a program called *Live Food for Live People* on cable television in Los Angeles, in the late 1980s, and his Busy Bee Hardware store (open since 1922), is almost certainly the only hardware store in the world that sells books on raw food. In 1995, Kidson opened his home to the public for lectures, raw potlucks, and meals. The Living Light House, as it was called, became a launching pad for several raw chefs and exposed many to the concept of living foods.

Deep Dish Spinach Pizza

MAKES 4 TO 6 SERVINGS

The chewy almond crust on this pizza is topped with fresh baby spinach and a thick cheesy sauce.

FOR THE CRUST

1½ cups almond pulp (see Almond Milk, page 24)

1 cup flaxseeds, ground in a high speed blender

¾ cup olive oil

⅓ cup fresh lemon juice

⅓ cup pure water

1½ cloves garlic, peeled

2 teaspoons dried thyme

2 teaspoons dried oregano

1¼ teaspoons dried sage

1¼ teaspoons dried rosemary

1¼ teaspoons sea salt

FOR THE CHEESE SAUCE

1¼ cups raw cashews

¾ cup chopped red bell peppers

6½ tablespoons coconut aminos

Generous 3 tablespoons fresh lemon juice

1 clove garlic, peeled

1 cup chopped spinach leaves

To make the crust, combine all of the ingredients in a mixing bowl. Knead the mixture by hand until a consistent, doughy texture is achieved. Spread mixture approximately ½ inch thick on a dehydrator tray lined with a Teflex sheet. Dehydrate one side at 105°F for 12 to 14 hours. Flip the bread onto a second dehydrator tray, peel off the Teflex sheet, and dehydrate for an additional 6 to 8 hours.

To make the sauce, in a high speed blender, combine all of the ingredients except the spinach and blend until smooth. Stir in the chopped spinach.

To assemble the pizza, leaving the crust on the mesh dehydrator sheet, spread the cheese sauce onto the crust as thickly as possible. Return the pizza to the dehydrator for an additional 1 to 2 hours, until the cheese begins to crisp along the top.

Cut into pizza-style triangles or squares and serve. Garnish with extra spinach leaves, lightly marinated in olive oil.

RAWVOLUTIONARY HEROES

David Jubb and **Annie Padden Jubb** are co-authors of *LifeFood Recipe Book* and *Secrets of an Alkaline Body*. Throughout the '90s, they lead fasts, lectured, and co-hosted *Universe Inside Our Mind,* a program on Manhattan cable television that promoted Lifefood. The Jubbs also founded their New York City café, Jubb's Longevity, in 2001. Dr. David Jubb has since written *Jubb's Cell Rejuvenation* and Annie Padden Jubb opened LifeFood Organic, a raw café in Los Angeles.

ENTRÉES

Falafel Wraps

MAKES 2 WRAPS

These wraps are fun to make and features our yummy carrot falafel balls.

FOR THE FALAFEL

1¼ cups shredded carrots

½ cup raw almonds

¼ cup chopped stemmed parsley

2½ tablespoons flaxseeds, ground in a
high speed blender

2½ tablespoons olive oil

2 tablespoons minced yellow onion

1 tablespoon fresh lemon juice

1 clove garlic, peeled

½ teaspoon sea salt

FOR THE WRAPS

½ cup Red Pepper Hummus (page 130)

2 large collard leaves, stems removed

½ cup chopped tomato

¼ cup diced red onion

½ cup stemmed mint leaves

¼ cup chopped raw black olives

To make the falafel, combine all of the ingredients in a food processor and process until homogenized. Scoop out approximately ⅓ cup of the mixture using a lever-style ice cream scoop. Place on a dehydrator sheet. Continue creating scoops from the remaining mixture. Dehydrate for 14 to 16 hours at 105°F. Remove from the dehydrator and refrigerate until ready to serve.

To assemble the wraps, spread ¼ cup of hummus along the center line of 1 collard leaf. Layer half of the tomato, red onion, mint leaves, and black olives on top of the hummus. Place half of the falafel balls on last. Repeat to make an additional wrap.

RAWVOLUTIONARY HERO

Gabriel Cousens is an American physician and homeopath who advocates live foods therapy. He is the director and founder of the Tree of Life Rejuvenation Center in Arizona, where he conducts scientific research on the effects of live food nutrition. Dr. Cousens is considered the leading live-foods medical doctor and has authored several books including *Spiritual Nutrition*, *Conscious Eating*, and *There Is a Cure for Diabetes*.

Green Dragon Rolls

 1 **B**

MAKES 4 ROLLS; 8 PIECES

Deliciously simple rolls filled with fresh baby greens, avocado, and our popular Garlic Cream Dressing.

4 sheets nori

2 cups baby greens

1 cup Garlic Cream Dressing (page 27)

1 avocado, sliced into spears

Lay out 1 nori sheet on a clean, dry surface. Place ½ cup of the greens in a narrow layer along the length of the nori sheet, about ½ inch from the edge closest to you. Spoon 1 tablespoon of the dressing across the top of the greens. Layer one-fourth of the avocado spears along the top, keeping all the ingredients in a narrow line. Fold the edge of the nori closest to you over the filling. Gently roll the nori away from you, tightly and evenly, into a firm, snugly wrapped roll. Seal the exposed edge of the nori to the roll by wetting it with pure water or dressing. Repeat to make 3 more rolls.

Cut each roll along a diagonal into 2 pieces with a sharp knife. Serve immediately with the remaining dressing as a dipping sauce.

RAWVOLUTIONARY HERO

Vivian Virginia Vetrano, a protégé of Herbert Shelton, is a leading authority on the alternative medicine philosophy Natural Hygiene. She is the author of several books including *Genuine Fruitarianism* and *Fruit Phobia.* Dr. Vetrano writes: "Heating any food destroys much of its vitamin, mineral, and protein content even as poisonous inorganic acids are formed. The all uncooked diet is most healthful."

Green Enchiladas

MAKES 2 ENCHILADAS

Our light and tangy green coconut wrap makes for a fantastic enchilada.

FOR THE CILANTRO WRAPS

2½ cups fresh coconut meat (see Note)

1 cup stemmed cilantro

1 cup spinach leaves

¼ cup chopped green onions

¼ cup coconut water

1 tablespoon fresh lemon juice

1 tablespoon coconut aminos

1½ jalapeños, halved and seeded

2 cloves garlic, peeled

Pinch of sea salt

FOR THE MANGO SALSA

⅔ cup chopped mango

⅔ cup chopped red bell pepper

⅔ cup chopped peeled cucumber

3 tablespoons minced seeded jalapeños

4 teaspoons fresh lemon or lime juice

1 teaspoon ground cumin

⅓ teaspoon sea salt

FOR THE ENCHILADAS

1½ cups chopped romaine leaves

1½ cups Taco Meat (page 32)

¼ cup Mayo (page 29)

½ avocado, diced

To make the wraps, in a high speed blender, combine all of the ingredients and blend until smooth. Spread the mixture thinly onto a dehydrator tray lined with a dehydrator sheet. Dehydrate one side at 105°F for 12 to 14 hours. Flip the bread onto a second dehydrator tray, peel off the Teflex, and dehydrate for an additional 4 hours. Cut into 4 equal squares. Store in a cool, dry place until ready to serve.

To make the salsa, combine all of the ingredients in a small mixing bowl and mix well.

To assemble the enchiladas, place ¾ cup of the chopped romaine on the plate in a square shape. Pile ¾ cup of the Taco Meat in a thick line down the center of the lettuce. Top the Taco Meat with a thick layer of mango salsa. Place the cilantro wrap over the Taco Meat, salsa, and lettuce, tucking it around the edges of the pile. Layer the top of the enchilada with 2 tablespoons of Mayo and some diced avocado. Repeat to make another enchilada. Serve immediately.

NOTE: If coconut meat is on the dry side, add a small amount of pure water or coconut water to make the consistency more spreadable.

Holy Macro Bowl

Our homage to macrobiotic cooking features kale, arame, red pepper tahini dressing, black sesame seeds, and our cashew Nofu.

FOR THE RED PEPPER TAHINI DRESSING

2 cups chopped red bell pepper

2 cups chopped carrot

¾ cup raw tahini

¼ cup apple cider vinegar

FOR THE SALAD

6 cups Simple Kale Salad (page 155)

A 4 by 4-inch block of Nofu (page 29), cubed into bite-size pieces

1 cup arame soaked for 15 minutes in pure water, then drained

Black sesame seeds, for garnish

To make the dressing, in a high speed blender, combine all of the ingredients and blend until smooth.

To make the salad, place 1½ to 3 cups of the kale salad in each salad bowl. Layer with the dressing, the Nofu cubes, and the arame. Garnish with the black sesame seeds.

RAWVOLUTIONARY HERO

Douglas Graham is an American Doctor of Chiropractic, a proponent of Natural Hygiene, and raw foodist since 1978. Dr. Graham is the author of several books that promote a raw foods way of life including *The 80/10/10 Diet,* which promotes the eating of mono meals, in the proportions of 80 percent carbohydrates, 10 percent protein, and 10 percent fat. Dr. Graham also lectures internationally on raw food nutrition.

Indonesian Noodle Affair

⬤2 ■B

MAKES 2 OR 3 SERVINGS

Kelp noodles are amazing when served with this cashew coconut paprika sauce.

FOR THE CHILI SAUCE

3¾ cups raw cashews

2 tablespoons coconut nectar

1½ tablespoons coconut aminos

1½ tablespoons apple cider vinegar

1 teaspoon Irish Moss Gel (see sidebar, page 29)

1 clove garlic, peeled

Pinch of ground cayenne

½ cup pure water

FOR THE NOODLES

6 cups kelp noodles

2 cups chopped baby bok choy

1 sheet nori, cut into ribbons

¼ cup black sesame seeds

1 red bell pepper, thinly sliced

¼ cup paprika sauce (see page 135)

To make the paprika sauce, in a high speed blender, combine all of the ingredients and blend until smooth.

To serve the noodles, toss the chili sauce with the kelp noodles and the bok choy in a large bowl until evenly coated. Place in serving bowls and garnish with the nori, black sesame seeds, and sliced bell pepper and top with a drizzle of paprika sauce. Serve immediately.

RAWVOLUTIONARY HERO

Phyllis Avery is a long-time practitioner of Natural Hygiene and contemporary of the late T. C. Fry. In her 1992 book, *The Garden of Eden Raw Fruit and Vegetable Recipes*, she wrote: "Man's physical and mental problems began when his diet changed from raw fruits, vegetables, nuts and seeds to cooked vegetables, flesh and grains."

Mediterranean Burgers

MAKES 4 BURGERS

Our classic burger patties are topped with rich hummus, raw green olives, and cashew feta.

- 8 green leaf lettuce leaves
- 8 slices RAWvolution's Famous Onion Bread (page 30)
- 4 Burger Patties (page 26)
- 1 cup Red Pepper Hummus (page 130)

- 4 thin slices red onion
- 12 raw green olives, thinly sliced
- Cashew feta (see Nofu, page 29), cut into 4 by 4-inch cubes

Place 2 lettuce leaves on a slice of RAWvolution's Famous Onion Bread. Set a burger patty on top of the lettuce and layer 3 or 4 tablespoons of hummus on top. Layer with onion, green olives, and cashew feta, and top with another slice of RAWvolution's Famous Onion Bread. Repeat to make 4 sandwiches.

RAWVOLUTIONARY HERO

Humbart Santillo is an American Doctor of Naturopathy and Master Herbalist who, after transitioning to a diet of mostly raw vegan foods, claims to have eliminated the chronic health problems that troubled him throughout his youth. In his 1993 book, *Food Enzymes,* Santillo wrote: "The difference between live (raw) food and dead food is enzymatic activity. If you had two seeds and boiled one, which one would grow when placed in the soil?"

Mexican Pizzas

MAKES 2 SERVINGS

This crispy, cheesy nori is topped with all your Mexican faves.

FOR THE CHEESY NORI CRISPS

2 sheets nori

⅔ cup cheese sauce (see Vegetable Casserole, page 206)

FOR THE PIZZA TOPPINGS

1 cup Taco Meat (page 32)

½ cup Guacamole (page 28)

½ cup Salsa (page 31)

2 tablespoons Mayo (page 29)

1 tablespoon minced stemmed cilantro

To make the nori crisps, spread ⅓ cup of the cheese sauce on each sheet of nori. Spread from the center outward, leaving a border of uncovered nori about ¼ inch wide all around. Fold up the uncovered edges, creating a slight lip. Place on a dehydrator tray and dehydrate for 12 hours at 105°F.

To assemble the pizzas, top the dehydrated cheesy nori crisps with layers of Taco Meat, Guacamole, Salsa, and a dollop of Mayo. Garnish with the cilantro. Serve immediately.

NOTE: Make extra cheesy nori crisps because they make great snacks when eaten plain or cut into chips.

RAWVOLUTIONARY HERO

Linda Goodman is a *New York Times* bestselling author and was known as the world's foremost authority on astrology. Goodman is credited with accelerating the growth of the New Age movement through the unprecedented success of her book *Linda Goodman's Sun Signs* (circa 1968). There are now over sixty million copies of Linda's books in print throughout the world! In 1993's *Star Signs*, Goodman states: "It's good to become a vegetarian, but the ultimate goal is to become a fruitarian . . ."

Mole Tacos

MAKES 8 TACOS

Nori taco shells are stuffed with spiced walnut meat, Guacamole, and a raw chocolate mole sauce.

FOR THE MOLE SAUCE

1 cup chopped tomatoes

¼ cup chopped red bell pepper

¼ cup sun dried tomatoes

4 teaspoons chili powder

2 teaspoons cacao powder

1 teaspoon sea salt

FOR THE TACOS

4 sheets nori, cut into taco shell shapes
(see Note)

2 cups Taco Meat (page 32)

2 cups Guacamole (page 28)

1 cup Seed Cheese (page 31)

1 cup Mayo (page 29)

To make the sauce, in a high speed blender, blend all of the ingredients until completely smooth.

To assemble the tacos, hold one nori taco shell open and layer in the Taco Meat, mole sauce, Guacamole, Seed Cheese, and Mayo inside. Repeat to make 7 more tacos. Serve immediately.

NOTE: To cut the nori into taco shell shapes, fold each sheet in half and cut 2 half circles from the center line of the fold. The circles should be approximately 5 inches in diameter.

RAWVOLUTIONARY HERO

Bob Dagger is the founder and owner of New York City's High Vibe, the first shop of its kind in the United States, and likely the world. Since 1993, High Vibe has been providing support products for the raw and living foods lifestyle, such as packaged raw foods, books, appliances, whole food supplements, and natural body care products.

Mock Chicken Sandwiches

MAKES 6 SANDWICHES

Dehydrated sunflower seed patties topped with cashew Mayo, heirloom tomatoes, and sunflower sprouts on our crispy RAWvolution's Famous Onion Bread.

FOR THE MOCK CHICKEN PATTIES

5½ cups Mayo (page 29)

3 cups soaked raw sunflower seeds (see Note), ground in a food processor

3 or 4 stalks celery, diced

½ bunch green onions, diced

2 tablespoons dried oregano

2 tablespoons dried sage

2 tablespoons dried thyme

FOR THE SANDWICHES

12 slices RAWvolution's Famous Onion Bread (page 30)

½ cup Mayo (page 29)

2 tomatoes, sliced

12 thin slices yellow onion

Clover or other sprouts

To make the patties, in a mixing bowl, combine all of the ingredients and mix well. Form the mixture into 6 round patties approximately ½ inch thick and 3 inches in diameter.

Dehydrate on a dehydrator tray lined with a Teflex sheet for 12 hours at 105°F. Flip the patties onto a second dehydrator tray, peel off the Teflex sheet, and dehydrate for an additional 12 hours, or until dry throughout. Store in a cool, dry place until ready to serve.

To assemble the sandwiches, on a slice of RAWvolution's Famous Onion Bread, layer with one sixth of the Mayo and the sprouts, 1 mock chicken patty, and one sixth of the tomato and onion slices. Top with another slice of Onion Bread. Repeat to make 5 more sandwiches.

NOTE: Soak the sunflower seeds in pure water for 2 to 4 hours then thoroughly drain.

RAWVOLUTIONARY HERO

Karl Eimer was a professor and the director of the Medical Clinic at the University of Vienna who studied the effect of a fully raw diet on athletes. Without exception, the athletes demonstrated improvements in reflex, speed, flexibility, and stamina after adopting an exclusively raw diet. Eimer concluded that raw foods increase cellular respiration and efficiency. His findings were reported in July of 1993.

Mock Turkey Sandwiches

MAKES 4 SANDWICHES

Our mock turkey is made from crispy, seasoned coconut meat and is perfect on a sandwich around Thanksgiving or any time of year.

FOR THE MOCK TURKEY

4 cups coconut meat

3 tablespoons olive oil

3 tablespoons porcini mushroom powder

1½ tablespoons coconut aminos

1½ tablespoons fresh lemon juice

1½ tablespoons dried sage

1½ tablespoons dried rosemary

FOR THE SANDWICHES

8 leaves green leaf lettuce

8 slices RAWvolution's Famous Onion Bread (page 30)

½ cup Mayo (page 29)

2 tomatoes, thinly sliced

To make the mock turkey, cut the coconut meat into thin strips, approximately 1 by 3 inches. In a mixing bowl, combine all of the ingredients and mix well. Cover and refrigerate. Allow the coconut meat to marinate like this for 2 to 4 hours. The longer it marinates, the richer the flavor will be.

Place the meat on a dehydrator tray with a Teflex sheet and dehydrate for 12 to 14 hours at 105°F. The texture will be great for sandwiches at this point. If you prefer a drier consistency, remove the Teflex sheet and dehydrate for an additional 6 to 8 hours.

To assemble the sandwiches, on a slice of Onion Bread, layer one fourth of the Mayo, 2 lettuce leaves, and one fourth of the tomato and mock turkey strips. Top with another slice of Onion Bread. Repeat to make 3 more sandwiches.

RAWVOLUTIONARY HERO

Art Baker is the author of 1994's *Awakening Our Self-Healing Body* in which he writes: "Overly cooked foods literally wreck our body. They deny needed nutrients to the system since heat alters foodstuffs such that they are partially, mostly, or wholly destroyed."

RAWVOLUTIONARY HERO

John McCabe is the author of *Sunfood Living, Sunfood Traveler, Igniting Your Life,* and *Sunfood Diet Infusion,* as well as other titles. He has also contributed to, edited, and ghostwritten numerous other books on raw food.

Mushroom Swiss Burgers

MAKES 4 BURGERS

Our classic walnut and sunflower burger patties are topped with marinated mushrooms and sunflower Seed Cheese.

- 8 green leaf lettuce leaves
- 8 slices RAWvolution's Famous Onion Bread (page 30)
- 4 Burger Patties (page 26)
- 1 cup Seed Cheese (page 31)

- 8 thin slices yellow onion
- 2 cups sliced button mushrooms marinated in about ½ cup Garlic Cream Dressing (page 27)

Place 2 leaves of green leaf lettuce on a slice of RAWvolution's Famous Onion Bread, layer with a patty, Seed Cheese, onion, and marinated mushrooms. Top the burger with another slice of Onion Bread. Repeat to make 3 more burgers.

RAWVOLUTIONARY HERO

Joel Fuhrman is an American physician who specializes in nutrition-based treatments for obesity and chronic disease. In his 1995 book, *Fasting and Eating for Health,* he states: "The more leafy green vegetables consumed in the diet, the longer the life span. This confirms the importance of raw, natural plant foods, the loss of important factors with cooking, and the protective effect of all the health-giving nutrients they contain."

Pesto Pizzas

MAKES 2 SERVINGS

Our legendary Onion Bread serves as the thin and crispy crust topped with fresh Pesto and baby greens in this savory pizza.

1 cup Pesto (page 30)

2 slices RAWvolution's Famous Onion Bread (page 30)

½ cup Mayo (page 29)

½ cup baby greens

Spread a thick layer of Pesto on each slice of RAWvolution's Famous Onion Bread. Spread Mayo on top of the Pesto and garnish with baby greens. Cut into pizza-style triangles or squares and serve.

RAWVOLUTIONARY HERO

Juliano is a pioneering raw food chef who virtually invented the concept of gourmet raw food as we know it. Juliano opened his first raw food restaurant in San Francisco, in the mid 1990s and later opened one in Los Angeles. Juliano is also the author of *Raw: The Uncook Book* (1999), the first guide to preparing gourmet raw cuisine released by a major publisher.

Pad Thai

MAKES 2 OR 3 SERVINGS .... 2 B

Kelp noodles in a spicy almond butter chile sauce topped with delicious cashew egg.

FOR THE PAD THAI SAUCE

- 1 cup raw almond butter
- 1 cup raw tahini
- 1 cup pure water
- ½ cup coconut aminos
- ¼ cup apple cider vinegar

- 4-inch piece peeled fresh ginger
- 6 cloves garlic, peeled
- 1 tablespoon coconut nectar
- 2 teaspoons ground cayenne
- 1 tablespoon sea salt

FOR THE PAD THAI

- 6 cups kelp noodles
- ⅔ cup Faux Egg (page 27), cashews, strips fresh coconut meat, thinly

- sliced red onion, sliced red bell pepper, and fresh mint leaves

To make the sauce, in a high speed blender, combine all of the ingredients and blend until smooth.

To make the Pad Thai, toss the sauce with the kelp noodles until evenly coated. Place in serving bowls and garnish with Faux Egg, cashews, fresh coconut, red onion, red bell pepper, and mint. Serve immediately.

RAWVOLUTIONARY HERO

David Wolfe is a world-renowned author and lecturer on raw food nutrition, superfoods, and longevity. He is the author of several books, including *The Sunfood Diet Success System, Eating for Beauty, Naked Chocolate, Superfoods,* and *Chaga.* Wolfe has hosted raw food adventure retreats worldwide, gives hundreds of lectures yearly, and is known for bringing raw cacao products, goji berries, and other superfoods into mainstream awareness and distribution throughout North America.

ENTRÉES

Red Enchiladas

MAKES 4 SERVINGS

These spicy chile and cilantro wraps are stuffed with oregano cheese and topped with avocado and a mango salsa.

FOR THE CHILI ANCHO WRAPS

- 2 cups fresh coconut meat (see Note)
- 4 teaspoons ancho chile powder
- 2 teaspoons coconut aminos
- 2 teaspoons olive oil
- 2 teaspoons sea salt
- 1⅓ teaspoons fresh lemon juice
- 1 teaspoon cumin powder
- 1 clove garlic, peeled
- 5 tablespoons stemmed cilantro, chopped

FOR THE ENCHILADA SAUCE

- 3 cups chopped tomatoes
- 5 tablespoons olive oil
- 2 tablespoons chili powder
- 1 tablespoon dried oregano
- 4½ teaspoons cumin powder
- 1 tablespoon sea salt
- 4 cloves garlic, peeled

FOR THE OREGANO CHEESE

- 3 cups raw cashews
- ½ cup fresh lemon juice
- 3 tablespoons Irish Moss Gel (see sidebar, page 29)
- 1 teaspoon sea salt
- 2 tablespoons fresh stemmed oregano

FOR THE MANGO SALSA

- ⅔ cup diced mango
- ⅔ cup diced red bell pepper
- ⅔ cup diced peeled cucumber
- 3 tablespoons minced seeded jalapeños
- 4 teaspoons fresh lemon or lime juice
- 1 teaspoon cumin powder
- ⅓ teaspoon sea salt

FOR THE ENCHILADAS

- 3 cups chopped romaine lettuce leaves
- 1 avocado, sliced

To make the wraps, in a high speed blender, combine all of the ingredients except the cilantro and blend until smooth. Stir in the cilantro. Spread a very thin layer of the mixture onto a dehydrator tray lined with a Teflex sheet. Dehydrate one side at 105°F for 12 to 14 hours. Flip onto a second dehydrator tray, peel off the Teflex sheet, and dehydrate for an additional 4 hours, or until completely dry. Cut into 4 equal squares. Store in a cool, dry place.

To make the enchilada sauce, in a high speed blender, combine all of the ingredients and blend until smooth.

To make the oregano cheese, in a high speed blender, combine all of the ingredients except the oregano and blend until smooth. Stir in the oregano.

To make the salsa, combine all of the ingredients in a small mixing bowl and mix well.

To assemble the enchiladas, place ¾ cup of the romaine on a plate in a square shape. Spread ¾ cup of oregano cheese in a thick line down the center of 1 wrap. Flip the wrap over and place, cheese side down, on top of the lettuce. Spoon the enchilada sauce on top of the enchilada and top with 4 thin slices of avocado and some mango salsa. Repeat to make 3 more enchiladas.

NOTE: If the coconut meat is on the dry side, add a small amount of pure water or coconut water to make the consistency more spreadable.

RAWVOLUTIONARY HERO

Thor Bazler (aka Stephen Arlin) was co-founder of Nature's First Law, one of the first raw foods distribution companies, and author of *Raw Power! Building Muscle & Strength Naturally*, the first book to incorporate raw foods and bodybuilding.

Reuben Sandwiches

MAKES 6 SANDWICHES

Specially seasoned patties topped with raw kraut and our own Thousand Island dressing are served between two pieces of our famous Onion Bread.

FOR THE RUEBEN PATTIES

½ cup soaked raw walnuts

¼ cup soaked raw almonds

¼ cup soaked raw sunflower seeds

1⅓ cups mushrooms, briefly marinated in 3 tablespoons coconut aminos

1 cup chopped celery

⅓ cup chopped yellow onion

¼ cup flaxseeds, ground in a high speed blender

¼ cup coconut aminos

3¼ tablespoons olive oil

3 tablespoons fresh thyme leaves

3 cloves garlic, peeled

4 teaspoons ground black pepper

4 teaspoons ground cloves

4 teaspoons crushed juniper berries

2½ teaspoons ground allspice

FOR THE THOUSAND ISLAND DRESSING

1 cup coconut water

¾ cup raw cashews

½ cup chopped red bell pepper

⅓ cup chopped raw pickles

¼ cup sun dried tomatoes

2 tablespoons fresh lemon juice

1 tablespoon minced yellow onion

4 teaspoons apple cider vinegar

1 teaspoon coconut nectar

2 cloves garlic, peeled

½ teaspoon sea salt

FOR THE SANDWICHES

½ cup stone-ground mustard

12 slices RAWvolution's Famous Onion Bread (page 30)

1 cup raw sauerkraut (store-bought or homemade)

To make the patties, grind the walnuts, almonds, and sunflower seeds in a food processor. Transfer to a mixing bowl, add the remaining ingredients, and mix thoroughly, making sure to break apart any lumps.

Form the mixture into round patties approximately ½ inch thick and 3 inches in diameter. Dehydrate on a dehydrator tray lined with a Teflex sheet for 12 hours at 105°F. Flip them onto a second dehydrator tray, peel off the Teflex sheet, and dehydrate for an additional 12 to 14 hours, or until thoroughly dry. Store in a cool, dry place.

To make the dressing, in a high speed blender, combine all of the ingredients and blend until smooth.

To assemble the sandwiches, spread mustard on 1 slice of RAWvolution's Famous Onion Bread, layer with a Reuben patty and some sauerkraut and top with Thousand Island dressing. Top the sandwich with another piece of Onion Bread. Repeat to make 5 more sandwiches.

Spicy Chipotle Burgers

MAKES 4 BURGERS

These burgers are for spice fanatics only. Prepare to be transported to hot sauce heaven!

FOR THE NUT-FREE BURGER PATTIES

- ¾ cup raw sunflower seeds, soaked in pure water for 3 to 4 hours and drained
- 6 tablespoons hemp seeds
- Generous ½ cup chopped portobello mushrooms, briefly marinated in 1½ to 2 tablespoons coconut aminos
- ½ cup flaxseeds, ground in a high speed blender
- ¾ cup chopped celery

- ¼ cup diced yellow onion
- 2 tablespoons chopped stemmed parsley
- 2 cloves garlic, minced
- ¼ cup coconut aminos
- 1¼ cups olive oil
- 1½ teaspoons cumin seeds
- Leaves from a few sprigs fresh tarragon, chopped
- ⅛ teaspoon cayenne

FOR THE CHIPOTLE SAUCE

- ½ cup apple cider vinegar
- ½ cup chopped red bell pepper
- ¼ cup chopped fresh parsley
- 3 tablespoons yacon syrup

- 2 tablespoons crushed chipotle pepper
- 1 tablespoon chopped yellow onion
- 1 tablespoon fresh lemon juice
- 1 clove garlic, peeled

FOR THE BURGERS

- 8 leaves red leaf lettuce
- 8 slices RAWvolution's Famous Onion Bread (page 30)
- 1 large tomato, sliced

- 4 thin slices yellow onion
- 1 cup cheese sauce (see Vegetable Casserole, page 206)

In a high-speed blender, grind the flaxseeds. To make the patties, using a food processor, grind the hemp seeds and sunflower seeds. Transfer all of the ingredients to a mixing bowl, add the remaining ingredients, and mix thoroughly, making sure to break apart any lumps.

Form the mixture by hand into round patties approximately ½ inch thick and 3 inches in diameter. Place the patties on a dehydrator tray lined with a Teflex sheet and dehydrate for 12 hours at 105°F. Flip the tray over onto an empty dehydrator tray and gently peel the sheet off the patties. Return to the dehydrator for another 12 hours, or until dry throughout. Store in a cool, dry place.

To make the chipotle sauce, in a high speed blender, combine all of the ingredients and blend until smooth.

To assemble the burgers, place 2 leaves of lettuce on a slice of RAWvolution's Famous Onion Bread. Layer with tomato slices, onion, a burger patty, and cheese sauce and top with chipotle sauce. Top the sandwich with another slice of Onion Bread. Repeat to make 3 more burgers. Serve immediately.

Szechuan Noodles

2 B

MAKES 2 OR 3 SERVINGS

Perfect zucchini noodles and a vegetable medley in a smoky, spicy sauce.

FOR THE VEGETABLE MIX

1 cup chopped baby bok choy

½ cup chopped broccoli

¼ cup shredded peeled carrots

¼ cup shredded peeled daikon

¼ cup shredded purple cabbage

¼ cup diced red bell pepper

¼ cup shredded parsnips

2 tablespoons chopped stemmed parsley

2 tablespoons diagonally sliced green onions

3 tablespoons black sesame seeds

FOR THE SZECHUAN SAUCE

5 cups olive oil

½ cup coconut aminos

½ cup coconut nectar

¼ cup ume vinegar

10 cloves garlic, peeled

3 tablespoons garam masala

3 tablespoons chili powder

2 tablespoons turmeric

2 tablespoons sea salt

1 teaspoon cayenne

6 cups zucchini noodles (raw zucchini peeled and cut like spaghetti noodles with a Spirooli slicer according to manufacturer's instructions; see Note)

Raw cashews, for garnish

To mix the vegetables, combine all of the vegetables ingredients in a large bowl.

To make the sauce, in a high speed blender, combine all of the sauce ingredients and blend until smooth.

Add the sauce to the vegetables and toss until evenly coated. When ready to serve, pour the sauce and vegetables over bowls of the zucchini noodles. Garnish with the raw cashews and serve.

NOTE: The texture of zucchini noodles improves when they are left to sit in the open air at room temperature for 6 to 8 hours.

RAWVOLUTIONARY HERO

Karyn Calabrese opened her raw food restaurant, Karyn's Fresh Corner, in the mid 1990s. It is still uncooking today and is the longest running raw food restaurant extant. In a ground-breaking appearance, Calabrese discussed raw foods on *The Oprah Winfrey Show* and is the author of the book, *Soak Your Nuts,* a cleansing and detoxification guide with raw food recipes.

Tiger Rolls

MAKES 4 ROLLS

These creamy curry rolls are filled with marinated veggies and cashew sauce.

FOR THE TIGER SAUCE

3½ cups raw cashews

½ cup pure water

2 tablespoons coconut nectar

1½ tablespoons apple cider vinegar

1½ tablespoons coconut aminos

1 teaspoon Irish Moss Gel (see sidebar, page 29)

1 clove garlic, peeled

Pinch of cayenne

FOR THE MARINATED VEGETABLES

2 tablespoons shredded zucchini

2 tablespoons shredded carrot

2 tablespoons sliced red bell pepper

2 tablespoons chopped baby bok choy

2 tablespoons shredded cabbage

2 tablespoons baby broccoli florets

2 tablespoons shredded parsnip

2 tablespoons chopped green onion

FOR THE ROLLS

4 Yellow Wraps (page 32)

2 avocados, sliced into spears

To make the sauce, in a high speed blender, combine all of the ingredients and blend until smooth. Set aside 1 cup of the sauce for serving with the rolls.

For the vegetables, in a mixing bowl, toss the remaining sauce and vegetables together until evenly coated. To assemble the rolls, lay out 1 wrap on a clean, dry surface. Place a layer of marinated vegetables across the edge closest to you, about ½ inch in from the edge. Layer one-fourth of the avocado spears on top of the vegetables. Grasp the edge closest to you and roll the wrap closed. Repeat to make 3 more rolls.

Serve immediately with the remaining tiger sauce on the side for dipping the rolls.

RAWVOLUTIONARY HERO

David Klein, a Hygienic Doctor with a Ph.D. in Natural Health, is the director of the Colitis & Crohn's Health Recovery Center in Maui, Hawaii. Dr. Klein is also editor of *Vibrance* magazine (formerly *Living Nutrition*), the world's most-read raw food lifestyle magazine, and co-author, with the late T. C. Fry, of *Your Natural Diet: Alive Raw Foods.*

Vegetable Casserole

MAKES 10 TO 12 SERVINGS

A hearty casserole, kinda like the ones Mom used to make. Complete with layers of vegetables, gravy, bread crumbs, and cheese sauce.

FOR THE GRAVY

3 cups chopped mushrooms

¾ cup coconut water

¾ cup pure water

½ cup raw tahini

½ cup chopped carrot

2 stalks celery, chopped

¼ cup fresh lemon juice

¼ cup coconut aminos

¼ cup chopped yellow onion

6 cloves garlic, peeled

1 tablespoon sea salt

FOR THE CHEESE SAUCE

2 cups raw cashews

½ cup fresh lemon juice

½ cup pure water

¼ cup chopped red bell pepper

1 teaspoon ground turmeric

⅛ teaspoon sea salt

FOR THE MARINATED VEGETABLES

3 cups spinach leaves

3 cups chopped cauliflower florets

2 cups chopped broccoli

2 cups chopped celery

1½ cups chopped green onions

1 cup stemmed parsley

1 cup diced carrots

1 cup diced parsnips

FOR THE CRUST AND THE GARNISH

4 cups crumbled RAWvolution's Famous Onion Bread (page 30) or Rosemary Crackers (page 131)

Thinly sliced tomato

To make the gravy, in a high speed blender, combine all of the ingredients and blend until smooth.

To make the cheese sauce, in a high speed blender, combine all of the ingredients and blend until smooth.

To marinate the vegetables, in a mixing bowl, combine all of the vegetables with the gravy and throughly mix. Allow this to marinate for 15 to 20 minutes.

To make the crust, cover the bottom of a medium-size baking dish with a thin layer of the crumbled RAWvolution's Famous Onion Bread or Rosemary Crackers.

To assemble the casserole, spread a thick layer of the marinated vegetables on the crust. Spread a thick layer of cheese sauce on top of the marinated vegetables to completely cover. Place the casserole on a dehydrator sheet and dehydrate at 105°F for at least 4 hours.

Serve warm. Garnish with the sliced tomato.

Santorini Sandwiches

These delicious cream cheese sandwiches are filled with fresh cucumber, tomato, black olives, and sprouts.

1⅓ cups Cream Cheese (page 26)

8 slices RAWvolution's Famous Onion
    Bread (page 30)

2 tomatoes, sliced

½ red onion, thinly sliced

1 medium-size cucumber, peeled and
    sliced

¼ cup chopped raw black olives

Alfalfa or clover sprouts

Spread a thick layer of Cream Cheese on a slice of RAWvolution's Famous Onion Bread and layer with tomato, red onion, cucumber, black olives, and sprouts. Top with another slice of Onion Bread. Repeat to make 3 more sandwiches.

RAWVOLUTIONARY HERO

Sapoty Brook is an Australian scientist, engineer, and inventor, and the author of the 1996 book, *Eco-Eating: A Guide to Balanced Eating for Health & Vitality*. In it, he writes: "The structure of fruit involves an enormous amount of negentropy that the tree has extracted from sunlight. Food mutilated by heat loses negentropy and information, and the harmony and order in the molecular systems of the food is lost."

Kids' Faves

Children can really thrive on raw foods! We have found, however, that the secret to sharing raw foods with children is to never use the word "healthy." In that way, kids aren't so different from a lot of adults! The recipes in this chapter are the favorites of many of our young patrons. Your kids, too, will likely find something here they will love. But remember, children are often satisfied with the simplicity of sliced fruit, carrot, and celery sticks, or a handful of raw jungle peanuts. Engaging children in the process of food preparation encourages them to try new things and builds knowledge and confidence around healthful food. Raw food preparation is a great family activity and no one needs to be near a hot stove! Children will enjoy turning on the blender once it's full, or checking the dehydrator to see if the bananas have dried yet. Let them have fun creating their meals and allow them to experiment. You never know— the next great raw chef may be right there in your kitchen!

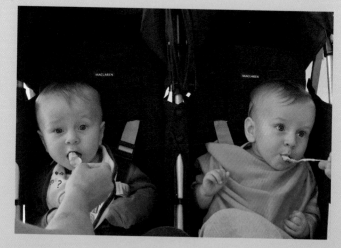

Almond Butter and Jelly Sandwiches

2 **P** **D**

MAKES 2 TO 4 SERVINGS

This scrumptious sandwich made with almond butter and raw strawberry jam is a real treat for kids of all ages.

½ cup fresh strawberries

2 tablespoons sun dried strawberries

4 slices Apple Bread (page 38)

½ cup raw almond butter

2 bananas, sliced

To make the strawberry jelly, in a high speed blender, combine the fresh strawberries and dried strawberries and blend until smooth.

Cut the Apple Bread slices in half, into triangles. Spread 2 tablespoons of the almond butter on each of 4 of the slices, top each with half of a sliced banana and 2 tablespoons of the jelly. Close up each sandwich with the remaining slices of bread and serve immediately.

Cheesy Broccoli

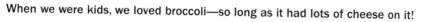

MAKES 2 SERVINGS ❶ **B**

When we were kids, we loved broccoli—so long as it had lots of cheese on it!

- 1 cup raw cashews
- ⅓ cup fresh lemon juice
- ⅓ cup pure water
- ¼ cup chopped red bell pepper

- 2 teaspoons nutritional yeast
- ⅓ teaspoon turmeric
- ½ teaspoon sea salt
- 3 cups broccoli florets and matchstick-cut broccoli stems

In a high speed blender, combine all of the ingredients except the broccoli and blend until smooth. In a mixing bowl, toss the broccoli with the cheese sauce until evenly coated.

SERVING SUGGESTION: For a more elegant presentation, substitute broccolini (also called "baby broccoli" and "aspiration") for the broccoli and layer the sauce instead of tossing.

Cheesy Kale Chips

MAKES 2 OR 3 SERVINGS

The tastiest way to eat lots of kale, these crispy chips are real winners.

FOR THE CHEESE SAUCE

⅓ cup fresh lemon juice

⅓ cup pure water

1 cup raw cashews

¼ cup chopped red bell pepper

⅓ teaspoon ground turmeric

½ teaspoon sea salt

2 teaspoons nutritional yeast

FOR THE MARINATED KALE

¾ teaspoon sea salt

9 cups torn stemmed kale

⅓ cup fresh lemon juice

To make the cheese sauce, in a high speed blender, combine all of the ingredients and blend until smooth.

To prepare the kale, in a large mixing bowl, massage the sea salt into the kale and let sit 10 minutes. Massage the lemon juice into the kale and let sit an additional 10 minutes.

Combine the kale with the cheese sauce until the kale is thoroughly coated. Spread the kale on a dehydrator tray and dehydrate for 24 hours at 105°F, or until crispy. Store in a zip-top bag or airtight container.

Dinosaur Kale Chips

MAKES 2 OR 3 SERVINGS

9 cups torn stemmed dinosaur or curly
   kale

¾ teaspoon sea salt

⅓ cup fresh lemon juice

¾ cup olive oil

⅓ cup coconut aminos

⅓ cup thinly sliced onion

½ clove garlic, minced

Pinch of ground cayenne

Pinch of ground cumin

In a large mixing bowl, massage the sea salt into the kale and let sit 10 minutes. Massage the lemon juice into the kale and let sit another 10 minutes. Mix in the remaining ingredients by hand. Refrigerate for 1 hour. Spread the kale on a dehydrator tray and dehydrate for 24 hours at 105°F, or until crispy. Store in a zip-top bag or airtight container.

Crunchings and Munchings Squash Seeds

1 **D**

MAKES 1 CUP

These salty seeds are easy to make and sure to please. We named them after a favorite phrase of Gurgi from the book *The Black Cauldron.*

1 cup fresh squash seeds (scraped from any variety of squash or pumpkin)

2 tablespoons olive oil

⅓ teaspoon sea salt

In a small mixing bowl, mix all of the ingredients until all of the seeds are evenly coated. Spread the seeds on a dehydrator tray and dehydrate for 12 to 20 hours at 105°F, until completely dry. Serve immediately or store in a cool, dry place.

Nana-choco-squiter

MAKES 2 SERVINGS

Bananas and chocolate sweetened with mesquite: What's not to love? We love to use mesquite as a simple sweetener in shakes and desserts. It's rich in minerals and low in sugar!

- **1½ cups coconut water**
- **1 cup nut milk (see Almond Milk, page 24)**

- **1 banana**
- **¼ cup cacao powder**
- **2 tablespoons mesquite powder**

In a high speed blender, combine all of the ingredients and blend until smooth.

SERVING SUGGESTION: Freeze the banana in advance to give the drink more of a milk shake texture.

KIDS' FAVES

Nuggy Buddies
Mock Chicken Nuggets

MAKES 12 NUGGETS

Bite-size sunflower nuggets with all of the essential sauces.

FOR THE MOCK CHICKEN

3 cups soaked raw sunflower seeds
(soaked for 2 to 4 hours and drained),
ground in a food processor

5¼ cups Mayo (page 29)

3 or 4 stalks celery, diced

½ bunch green onions, diced

2 tablespoons dried oregano

2 tablespoons dried sage

2 tablespoons dried thyme

¾ cup flaxseeds, ground in a high speed
blender

FOR THE BARBECUE SAUCE

½ cup sun dried tomatoes

⅓ cup freshly pureed tomatoes

2 teaspoons apple cider vinegar

1 teaspoon coconut aminos

1 teaspoon minced yellow onion

1 clove garlic, peeled

½ teaspoon chili powder

FOR THE CREAMY RANCH DRESSING

½ cup raw macadamia nuts, pine nuts,
or cashews

6 tablespoons coconut water

2½ tablespoons fresh lemon juice

1 clove garlic, peeled

¼ teaspoon sea salt

FOR THE SWEET MUSTARD SAUCE

Scant 1 cup stone-ground mustard

1 tablespoon coconut nectar

To make the mock chicken, in a large mixing bowl, combine all of the ingredients except the ground flaxseeds and mix well. Form into nugget-size pieces and roll each in the ground flaxseeds. Place on a dehydrator tray and dehydrate for 12 to 20 hours at 105°F, until dry on the outside and still slightly soft on the inside.

To make the barbecue sauce and creamy ranch dressing, combine each set of ingredients in a high speed blender and blend until smooth.

To make the sweet mustard, mix the mustard and coconut nectar by hand with a fork or spoon.

Serve the nuggets with your choice of dressing for dipping.

Tutti Frutti Fruit Chips

 D

MAKES 4 TO 6 SERVINGS

Apples, bananas, and pears, oh my!

3 pears, sliced

3 apples, cored and cut into flat rings

2 teaspoons ground cinnamon

In a mixing bowl, combine the apples, pears, and cinnamon and mix well. Spread on a dehydrator tray and dehydrate for 12 to 14 hours at 105°F. Store in a cool, dry place until ready to serve.

Rootin' Tootin' Root Veggie Chips

1 **D**

MAKES 4 TO 6 SERVINGS

These veggie chips are a terrific, healthy snack.

- **2 medium-size carrots, sliced**
- **1 medium-size beet, sliced**
- **2 tomatoes, sliced**
- **1 large zucchini, sliced**
- **2 medium-size parsnips, sliced**
- **⅓ cup olive oil**
- **1 teaspoon sea salt**

In a mixing bowl, combine the vegetables, olive oil, and sea salt and mix well. Spread the veggies on a mesh dehydrator sheet and dehydrate for 12 to 14 hours at 105°F. Store in a cool, dry place until ready to serve.

Desserts & Sweets

What's not to love about raw food desserts? Chocolate, fruit, nuts, and coconut are hard to argue with, even for the most diehard junk food enthusiast. These desserts taste so good, most won't even realize they're good *for* you! Bring our treats to any party or potluck and they might be gone before you even get to have some yourself.

Unfired confections will in time be as much in demand as candy is now.

—George Julius Drews, 1912

Almond Butter Cups

 2 **B**

MAKES 12 TO 14 CUPS

Delicious chocolates filled with almond butter.

1 cup melted Basic Chocolate (page 25)

12 to 14 almonds (optional)

2 pinches sea salt

⅓ cup raw almond butter

Pour ½ cup of the melted chocolate into the bottom of twelve to fourteen cups of a polycarbonate chocolate mold tray (see Note). (To present the almond butter cups with almonds on top, place an almond in the bottom of each cup before pouring the chocolate. Pour slowly so the almond stays in place.) Rock the mold tray from side to side so that the chocolate covers the inside edges of each cup. Put the mold tray in the refrigerator for approximately 15 minutes to harden the chocolate.

Add sea salt to the almond butter and mix well by hand.

After the chocolate has hardened, spoon approximately 1 teaspoon of the salted almond butter into the center of each cup.

Fill the cups with the remaining melted chocolate, ensuring that the filling is completely sealed in. Using a spatula, wipe the edges to remove and save any excess chocolate. Return the cups to the refrigerator for the chocolate to harden, about 15 minutes.

Gently knock the mold upside down against a clean work surface. The chocolate cups will fall out neatly. Store, covered, in the refrigerator until ready to serve.

NOTE: If you do not have a chocolate mold tray, it is very simple and fun to make a chocolate bark with this recipe instead. Pour the chocolate onto a small baking tray and spoon the almond butter evenly or unevenly across the top. Refrigerate the tray until the chocolate hardens. When ready to serve, cut pieces off or break into asymmetrical shapes.

RAWVOLUTIONARY HEROES

Jeremy Safron and Renée Loux (née Underkoffler) founded Hawaii's Raw Experience restaurant (1996–1999) and co-wrote *The Raw Truth,* one of the first contemporary raw food recipe books, in 1997. Safron and Loux have independently authored additional raw lifestyle books as well as books on related topics.

Banana Lickety Split

MAKES 1 BANANA SPLIT

Turn your raw ice cream into a banana split easily and deliciously.

2 or 3 scoops Vanilla Ice Cream
(page 235)

2 whole bananas, or 1 banana sliced
lengthwise

½ cup melted Basic Chocolate
(page 25)

2 tablespoons jungle peanuts, chopped
in a food processor

Lay the banana(s) in the bottom of a serving dish and place the scoops of ice cream on top. Add the chocolate sauce and the peanuts. Serve immediately.

Black and White Cookies

MAKES 6 OR 7 COOKIES

These simple almond and coconut cookies are flavored with vanilla beans and dipped in delicious chocolate.

- 2 cups almond pulp (see Almond Milk, page 24)
- 1 cup dried shredded coconut
- ½ cup coconut nectar
- ½ teaspoon vanilla bean powder
- 1 cup melted Basic Chocolate (page 25)

In a mixing bowl, combine the almond pulp, shredded coconut, coconut nectar, and vanilla bean powder. Knead until the mixture is homogenized. Scoop out approximately ¼ cup of the mixture, roll into a ball, and flatten into a cookie shape. Repeat to make 5 or 6 more cookies.

Place the cookies on a dehydrator tray and dehydrate at 105°F for 16 hours, or until thoroughly dry.

Dip one side of each cookie in the melted chocolate and lay on a baking tray, face up, to allow the chocolate to cool and dry. Refrigerate or freeze to help set the chocolate. Keep refrigerated until ready to serve.

Chocolate Buckwheat Tortugas

MAKES 8 TO 10 TURTLES

Sprouted buckwheat gives these little turtles their unique texture and satisfying crunch.

¾ cup dehydrated sprouted buckwheat (soaked for 2 to 4 hours, drained, and dehydrated for 48 hours at 105°F)

½ cup melted Basic Chocolate (page 25)

In a small mixing bowl, mix the sprouted buckwheat with the melted chocolate. While the chocolate is still liquid, pour the mixture into 8 to 10 cups of a polycarbonate chocolate turtle mold tray (see Note). Using a spatula, wipe the edges to remove and save any excess chocolate. Place the chocolates in the refrigerator for the chocolate to harden, about 20 minutes.

Gently knock the tray upside down against a clean work surface. The chocolates should fall out neatly. Cover and store in the refrigerator until ready to serve.

NOTE: If you do not have a chocolate turtle mold tray, it is very simple and fun to make a chocolate bark with this recipe instead. Pour the chocolate onto a small baking tray and spoon the sprouted buckwheat evenly or unevenly across the top. Refrigerate until the chocolate hardens. When ready to serve, cut pieces off or break into asymmetrical shapes.

RAWVOLUTIONARY HERO

Roe Gallo changed her diet to one of raw and living foods and reversed the chronic asthma she was told she would soon die from. Decades later, Gallo is an author and lecturer on raw food nutrition who, in 1997, wrote *Perfect Body*, a cleansing, detoxification, and raw foods lifestyle book.

Chocolate Chip Cookie Dough Balls

MAKES APPROXIMATELY 12 BALLS

Rich and buttery coconut cream balls, with cacao nibs and maca.

- 1 cup coconut butter
- ½ cup coconut nectar

- 2 tablespoons cacao nibs
- 2 tablespoons maca powder

Combine all of the ingredients in a bowl and knead the mixture by hand. Refrigerate until somewhat hardened, about 20 minutes. Scoop out 2 tablespoons and roll into a ball by hand. Use coconut oil on your hands to make the rolling smoother, if necessary. Continue rolling to make 11 more balls. Store refrigerated until ready to eat.

Chocolate Ganache Torte

MAKES 12 SERVINGS

This dark chocolate cake was created in heaven by raw pastry chef Krisztina Agramonte to be enjoyed one small slow bite at a time.

FOR THE TORTE CRUST

½ cup cacao nibs

¼ cup coconut sugar

Pinch of sea salt

Pinch of vanilla bean powder

FOR THE TORTE FILLING

8 cups raw cashews

2 cups coconut nectar

2 cups Almond Milk (page 24)

2 cups cacao powder

½ teaspoon vanilla bean powder

¼ teaspoon ground cinnamon

⅛ teaspoon grated nutmeg

⅛ teaspoon sea salt

1 cup coconut oil

1½ cups melted cacao butter

To make the crust, in a high speed blender, blend all of the ingredients into a semi-coarse powder. Sprinkle the crust generously into the bottom of a 9-inch springform cake pan.

To make the filling, in a high speed blender, combine all of the ingredients except the coconut oil and melted cacao butter and blend until smooth. Add the coconut oil and cacao butter only after the other ingredients are well-blended and blend again.

Pour the filling into the springform pan and place in the freezer. If you have any crust mixture remaining, use some to decorate the top of the cake. Torte will be completely set up and ready to serve in 12 hours.

Chocolate Ice Cream

MAKES 5 OR 6 SERVINGS

Make these delicious coconut and cashew ice creams and you'll never want store-bought again.

2 cups raw cashews

2 cups fresh coconut meat

1 cup cacao powder

1 cup coconut water

1 cup coconut nectar

¼ cup coconut oil

2½ tablespoons vanilla bean powder

½ teaspoon sea salt

In a high speed blender, combine all of the ingredients and blend until smooth. Refrigerate and process in an ice cream maker (see Note). Store in the freezer until ready to serve.

NOTE: If you don't have an ice cream maker, you can still make this recipe. Just blend it and freeze it. It won't be as fluffy as ice cream, but it will still be delicious.

Green Tea Ice Cream

MAKES 5 OR 6 SERVINGS

2 cups raw cashews

2 cups fresh coconut meat

1¼ cups coconut nectar

1 cup coconut water

¼ cup coconut oil

2½ tablespoons vanilla bean powder

2 tablespoons matcha green tea powder

½ teaspoon sea salt

In a high speed blender, combine all of the ingredients and blend until smooth. Refrigerate and process in an ice cream maker (or see Note, above). Store in the freezer until ready to serve.

RAWVOLUTIONARY HERO

Elysa Markowitz is the author of *Warming Up to Living Foods, Living with Green Power,* and *Smoothies* and hosted a public access television program in Los Angeles called *Elysa's Raw and Wild Food Show.*

Vanilla Ice Cream

2 B I

MAKES 5 OR 6 SERVINGS

2 cups raw cashews

2 cups fresh coconut meat

1 cup coconut water

1 cup coconut nectar

¼ cup coconut oil

2½ tablespoons vanilla bean powder

½ teaspoon sea salt

In a high speed blender, combine all of the ingredients and blend until smooth. Refrigerate and process in an ice cream maker (or see Note, page 232). Store in the freezer until ready to serve.

Cool Cherry Cream Parfaits

1 B

MAKES 2 SERVINGS

Coconut cream and fresh fruit make these parfaits popular sweet treats.

3½ cups coconut meat

½ cup coconut water

2 tablespoons coconut nectar

¾ cup chopped pitted cherries

Blend the coconut meat and coconut water together to make parfait cream. Layer the cream and cherries in 2 tall glasses. Chill before serving.

Fruit Tree Peach Cream Parfaits

1 B

MAKES 2 SERVINGS

3½ cups fresh coconut meat

½ cup coconut water

2 tablespoons coconut nectar

2 peaches, pitted and sliced

Blend the coconut meat and coconut water together to make parfait cream. Layer the cream and sliced peaches in 2 tall glasses. Chill before serving.

DESSERTS & SWEETS

Crystal Crunch Bars

MAKES 8 BARS

Sweet and tart, crunchy and creamy, this bar is pure bliss and loaded with antioxidant-rich berries.

FOR THE CRYSTAL CRUNCH GRANOLA MIX

¼ cup pomegranate powder

1¼ cups chopped raw walnuts

1¼ cups hemp seeds

1 cup sprouted buckwheat, soaked for
2 to 4 hours then drained

¾ cup shredded coconut

¾ cup chopped raw almonds

2 cups pureed raspberries

1¼ cups raisins

1 cup pureed blackberries

¾ cup chopped goldenberries

½ cup chopped mulberries

FOR THE CRYSTAL SYRUP

½ cup pomegranate powder

¼ cup coconut sugar

¼ cup coconut nectar

¼ cup coconut oil

2 teaspoons açaí berry powder

1 teaspoon vanilla bean powder

Pinch of sea salt

FOR THE DRIZZLE SAUCE

⅓ cup coconut oil

¼ cup fresh coconut meat

¼ cup raspberries or strawberries

2 tablespoons coconut nectar

To make the granola mix, in a large mixing bowl, combine all of the ingredients and mix them well. Spread the mixture on a dehydrator tray and dehydrate for approximately 48 hours at 105°F.

To make the syrup, in a high speed blender, combine all of the ingredients and blend until smooth.

To make the sauce, in a blender, combine all of the ingredients and blend until smooth.

In a large mixing bowl, combine the granola mix and crystal syrup. Mix together by hand until the granola is evenly coated with syrup.

Press the mixture into a small baking tray. Place the tray in the freezer for 30 minutes. Using a sharp knife, cut into 8 bars. Decorate the bars with the drizzle sauce and refrigerate until ready to serve.

Dark Chocolate Peanut Butter Bars

MAKES 10 TO 12 BARS

Sprouted buckwheat and jungle peanut butter enrobed in chocolate to perfection.

FOR THE FILLING

3 cups melted Basic Chocolate
  (page 25)

1¼ cups jungle peanuts

1 cup raw walnuts

1 cup dehydrated sprouted buckwheat
  (soaked for 2 to 4 hours, drained, and
  dehydrated for 48 hours at 105°F)

¼ cup raisins

¼ cup coconut nectar

¼ cup jungle peanut butter

¼ cup coconut oil

Pinch of vanilla bean powder

Pinch of sea salt

Pour 1½ cups of the melted chocolate into 10 to 12 cups of a polycarbonate chocolate mold tray (see Note). Rock the mold tray from side to side so that the chocolate covers the inside edges of each cup. Put the mold tray in the refrigerator for approximately 15 minutes to harden the chocolate.

In a food processor, mix the jungle peanuts, walnuts, sprouted buckwheat, raisins, coconut nectar, jungle peanut butter, coconut oil, vanilla bean powder, and sea salt until homogenized.

After the chocolate shell has hardened, spoon and spread approximately 1½ tablespoons of the peanut butter mixture along the center of each bar.

Fill the cups with the remaining melted chocolate, ensuring that the filling is completely sealed in. Using a spatula, wipe the edges to remove and save any excess chocolate. Return the tray to the refrigerator for the chocolate to harden, about 15 minutes.

Gently knock the tray upside down against a clean work surface. The bars should fall out neatly. Store, covered, in the refrigerator until ready to serve.

NOTE: If you do not have a chocolate mold tray, it is very simple and fun to make a chocolate bark with this recipe instead. Pour the chocolate onto a small baking tray, spoon the peanut filling onto the chocolate evenly or unevenly across the top. Refrigerate the tray until the chocolate hardens. When ready to serve, cut pieces off or break into asymmetrical shapes.

Chai Spider Ice Cream Float

MAKES 1 SERVING

Creamy cold chai splashed around homemade vanilla ice cream. An employee named this for a similar dish from her native Australia.

- ⅓ cup coconut butter
- 2-inch piece peeled fresh ginger
- 1 teaspoon grated nutmeg
- 1 teaspoon ground cardamom
- ½ teaspoon vanilla bean powder
- 4 teaspoons ground cinnamon
- 1 teaspoon ground black pepper
- ½ teaspoon ground cloves
- ¼ cup coconut nectar
- 1 cup nut milk (see Almond Milk, page 24)
- 2 scoops Vanilla Ice Cream (page 235)

To make the chai base, blend all of the ingredients except the ice cream in a high speed blender until smooth. Pour into a large glass mug, add the vanilla ice cream, and serve immediately.

RAWVOLUTIONARY HERO

Hygeia Halfmoon is an advocate for natural child care and is the author of *Primal Mothering in a Modern World,* in which she writes: "The key to success is massive raw foods action. In time, the rest will take care of itself."

Decadent Velvet Hot Chocolate

MAKES 2 SERVINGS

This dessert drink is truly decadent in every sense. Loads of chocolate and almond butter make it an experience.

- 2 cups hot pure water
- ½ cup nut milk (see Almond Milk, page 24)
- ½ cup coconut butter
- ½ cup cacao powder
- ¼ cup coconut nectar
- 2 tablespoons raw almond butter
- 1 teaspoon vanilla bean powder
- 1 teaspoon ground cinnamon
- ½ teaspoon ground cayenne

In a high speed blender, combine all of the ingredients and blend until smooth. Pour into mugs and serve while warm.

RAWVOLUTIONARY HERO

John Kohler turned to living foods in the mid-1990s after being diagnosed with spinal meningitis; he claims to have enjoyed dynamic health ever since. John is an expert on raw food appliances and gadgets, and is the founder and webmaster of living-foods.com, the largest living and raw food resource site on the internet.

Fluffy Pudding Parfaits

2 **B**

MAKES 2 SERVINGS

Chocolate- and strawberry-flavored rich almond and coconut puddings are heavenly.

FOR THE STRAWBERRY PUDDING

2½ cups coconut nectar

½ cup strawberries or fruit of your choice

2 tablespoons Irish Moss Gel (see sidebar, page 29)

2 tablespoons nut milk (see Almond Milk, page 24)

Dash of sea salt

1¼ cups fresh coconut meat

1 tablespoon coconut oil

FOR THE CHOCOLATE PUDDING

½ cup nut milk (see Almond Milk, page 24)

¼ cup coconut nectar

2 tablespoons Irish Moss Gel (see sidebar, page 29)

1 heaping tablespoon cacao powder

½ teaspoon vanilla bean powder

Dash of sea salt

1¼ cups fresh coconut meat

1 tablespoon coconut oil

To make the strawberry pudding, in a high speed blender, combine the coconut nectar, strawberries, Irish moss, nut milk, and sea salt and thoroughly blend. Add the coconut meat and blend again until smooth. Add the coconut oil and continue blending until thoroughly homogenized. Transfer the pudding to a container and refrigerate for 20 to 30 minutes.

To make the chocolate pudding, in a high speed blender, combine the nut milk, coconut nectar, Irish moss, cacao powder, vanilla powder, and salt and thoroughly blend. Add the coconut meat and blend until smooth. Add the coconut oil and continue blending until thoroughly homogenized. Transfer to a container and refrigerate for 20 to 30 minutes.

Spoon the strawberry and chocolate puddings into 2 glasses in alternating layers, or serve each flavor separately.

VARIATIONS: Make your own flavors by substituting ingredients like green tea powder, goji berries, pineapple juice, pomegranate powder, or whatever else you dream up.

RAWVOLUTIONARY HEROES

Richard DeAndrea, Woody Harrelson, and John Wood were part of Hollywood's O2 oxygen bar and raw food restaurant (1998–1999). Doctors DeAndrea and Wood later formulated the Dr. Greens Superfood powder and developed the 21 Day Detox program that ran in Los Angeles and San Francisco. They now offer autologous stem cell therapy in Thailand. Harrelson continues to be a very successful and well-respected Hollywood film actor and environmental activist.

Montelimat Espresso Bonbons

MAKES APPROXIMATELY 20 BONBONS

These bonbons have a delicious nutty filling flavored with our favorite hazelnut herbal coffee.

4 cups melted Basic Chocolate (page 25)

¼ cup cacao nibs (optional)

3 cups soaked raw cashews

1 cup coconut oil

1 cup Irish Moss Gel (see sidebar, page 29)

1 cup yacon syrup

¼ cup lucuma powder

6 tablespoons ground Teeccino herbal coffee

1 tablespoon vanilla bean powder

Pinch of sea salt

Pour 2 cups of the melted Basic Chocolate into approximately 20 cups of a polycarbonate bonbon mold tray (see Note). (To present the bonbons with cacao nibs on top, simply place cacao nibs in the bottom of each mold before pouring the chocolate. Pour slowly so the nibs stay in place.) Rock the tray from side to side so that the chocolate covers the inside edges of each cup. Refrigerate for approximately 15 minutes to harden the chocolate.

In a food processor, mix the cashews, coconut oil, Irish Moss Gel, yacon syrup, lucuma powder, herbal coffee, vanilla bean powder, and sea salt until homogenized.

After the chocolate shell has hardened, spoon and spread approximately 1 tablespoon of the filling in the center of each bonbon. Fill the cups with the remaining melted chocolate, ensuring that the filling is completely sealed in. Using a spatula, wipe the edges to remove and save any excess chocolate. Return the bonbons to the refrigerator to allow the chocolate to harden, about 15 minutes.

Gently knock the mold upside down against a clean work surface. The bonbons will fall out neatly. Store, covered, in the refrigerator until ready to serve.

NOTE: If you do not have a chocolate mold tray, it is very simple and fun to make a chocolate bark with this recipe instead. Pour the chocolate onto a small baking tray, spoon the espresso filling onto the chocolate evenly or unevenly across the top. Refrigerate the tray until the chocolate hardens. When ready to serve, cut pieces off or break into asymmetrical shapes.

RAWVOLUTIONARY HERO

Cherie Soria was a student of Ann Wigmore's and is the founder of the Living Light Culinary Institute, the world's first raw food preparation school, located in Northern California. Soria is co-author of *Angel Foods* and *The Raw Food Revolution Diet.*

Ninja Protein Balls

MAKES APPROXIMATELY 12 BALLS

Janabai used to mix all of the ingredients for this recipe in a bowl and eat it with a spoon before heading to yoga, the gym, or martial arts practice. She figured our customers would prefer something a little easier to eat on the go, so she started rolling Ninja Balls. Almond butter, green superfoods, and protein powder make these a perfect, quick energy boost.

1⅓ cups raw almond butter

½ cup dried shredded coconut

⅓ cup roughly chopped goji berries

¼ cup raw protein powder

2½ tablespoons cacao powder

2½ tablespoons Billy's Infinity Greens powder or green powder of your choice

1 tablespoon mesquite powder

5 teaspoons coconut nectar

5 teaspoons maca powder

4 teaspoons matcha green tea powder

¾ cup ground cacao nibs, ground in a high speed blender

In a large mixing bowl, combine all of the ingredients except the ground cacao nibs and mix well by hand. Scoop out 2 tablespoons and roll by hand to make a ball. Once formed, roll the ball in the ground cacao nibs. Repeat to make 11 more balls. Store in the refrigerator until ready to serve.

Peppermint Patties

MAKES APPROXIMATELY 20 PATTIES

These classic favorites are filled with a sweet and minty coconut cream.

FOR THE FILLING

2½ cups shredded coconut

6 tablespoons coconut oil

6 tablespoons coconut nectar

1 teaspoon vanilla bean powder

1 teaspoon liquid chlorophyll

6 to 8 drops food-grade peppermint essential oil

Pinch of sea salt

FOR THE ICING

1 cup fresh coconut meat

3 tablespoons coconut nectar

Dash of liquid chlorophyll

2 cups melted Basic Chocolate (page 25)

To make the filling, in a mixing bowl, mix all the ingredients by hand until evenly mixed.

To make the icing, in a high speed blender, combine all of the ingredients except the melted chocolate and blend until smooth.

Use the lid of a 32-ounce mason jar to form the patties to a consistent size: Place a piece of plastic wrap inside the lid and fill the lid with the patty filling. Pop out the patty using the plastic wrap. Place the patty on a baking tray covered in wax paper. Repeat to make about 19 more patties. Place the patties in the freezer for 15 to 20 minutes to give them time to solidify.

Dip one side of each patty in the melted chocolate and place, chocolate side up, on the baking tray. Return the patties to the refrigerator to harden, 30 minutes. Repeat to coat the other side of each patty. Refrigerate again to harden.

Spread a thin coat of icing on top of the patties. Refrigerate one final time to set the icing. Store the patties in the refrigerator until ready to serve.

RAWVOLUTIONARY HERO

Nomi Shannon is a certified Hippocrates Health Educator who has lived as a raw foodist since 1987. In 1999, *The Raw Gourmet*, her first collection of raw food recipes, was published.

Sugar-Free Chocolate Mousse

MAKES 2 SERVINGS

These light and creamy desserts are super tasty and super easy to make!

- 3 cups fresh coconut meat
- 2 tablespoons cacao powder
- 1 tablespoon mesquite powder
- ½ teaspoon vanilla bean powder
- 5 drops liquid stevia

In a high speed blender, combine all of the ingredients and blend until smooth. Refrigerate.

Sweet Emotions Vanilla Pudding

MAKES 2 SERVINGS

- 3 cups fresh coconut meat
- ¼ cup coconut water
- ¼ cup coconut nectar
- ½ teaspoon vanilla bean powder

In a high speed blender, combine all of the ingredients and blend until smooth. Refrigerate.

SERVING SUGGESTION: This pudding goes well with fresh berries.

RAWVOLUTIONARY HERO

William D. Scott, a Seventh-Day Adventist, wrote the 1999 book, *In the Beginning, God Said, Eat Raw Food.* In it, Scott describes his drastic change in lifestyle that brought about physical healing from the near-fatal illness he suffered and the degenerative disease that his wife struggled with.

Sweet Illusions Almond Bars

MAKES 4 TO 6 BARS

These coconut-filled chocolate and almond bars are sure to fill you with joy.

1½ cups melted Basic Chocolate
   (page 25)

12 to 18 almonds (optional)

2½ cups shredded coconut

½ cup coconut nectar

6 tablespoons coconut oil

½ teaspoon vanilla bean powder

Pinch of sea salt

Pour ¾ cup of the melted chocolate into the bottom of 4 to 6 cups of a polycarbonate chocolate bar mold tray (see Note). (To present the almond bars with whole almonds, simply place almonds in the bottom of each mold before pouring the chocolate. Pour slowly so the almonds stay in place.) Rock the mold tray from side to side so that the chocolate covers the inside edges of each cup. Refrigerate for approximately 15 minutes to harden the chocolate.

In a mixing bowl, mix the shredded coconut, coconut nectar, coconut oil, vanilla bean powder, and sea salt until mixed evenly.

After the chocolate has hardened, spoon and spread approximately 1½ tablespoons of the coconut mixture along the center of each bar. Fill the cups with the remaining melted chocolate, ensuring that the filling is completely sealed in. Using a spatula, wipe the edges to remove and save any excess chocolate. Return the bars to the refrigerator for the chocolate to harden, about 15 minutes.

Gently knock the mold upside down against a clean work surface. The bars should fall out neatly. Store, covered, in the refrigerator until ready to serve.

NOTE: If you do not have a chocolate mold tray, it is very simple and fun to make a chocolate bark with this recipe instead. Pour the chocolate onto a small baking tray and spoon the coconut filling onto the chocolate evenly or unevenly across the top. Refrigerate the tray until the chocolate hardens. When ready to serve, cut pieces off or break into asymmetrical shapes.

RAWVOLUTIONARY HEROES

Mun Chan and Dan Hoyt are the founders and owners of Quintessence, one of New York City's first raw food restaurants. Quintessence opened in 1999 and is still thriving today. Hoyt also teaches raw food preparation classes and has served as an international raw food restaurant consultant.

Mint Chocolate Hearts

MAKES APPROXIMATELY 10 HEARTS

We learned to make chocolates over the years with a little help from our friends. Thanks to Brian Waldrip and Jeffrey Botticelli!

8 to 10 drops food-grade peppermint essential oil

1¼ cups melted Basic Chocolate (page 25)

Mix the peppermint essential oil thoroughly into the melted chocolate. Pour the melted chocolate into 10 cups of a polycarbonate heart mold tray (see Note). Refrigerate for 25 to 30 minutes to harden the chocolate. Gently knock the tray upside down against a clean work surface. The hearts will fall out neatly. Store, covered, in the refrigerator until ready to serve.

NOTE: If you do not have a chocolate mold tray, it is very simple and fun to make a chocolate bark with this recipe instead. Pour the chocolate onto a small baking tray. Refrigerate the tray until the chocolate hardens. When ready to serve, cut pieces off or break into asymmetrical shapes.

Life

Sample Menus

Here, we offer fun pairings that can turn a raw meal into an extravagant, themed feast! And—you won't have to fall off the wagon when you have a craving for Mexican food!

Troph (trof), v. t. To prepare and combine provisions for the unfired diet; to make fruits, vegetables, and nuts palatable to be eaten unfired; to make an aesthetic display of wholesome unfired food; to entertain with the unfired fare; to serve unfired menus.

—term coined by George Julius Drews, 1912

AMERICAN

Vegetable Casserole (page 206)

Cheesy Broccoli (page 213)

Banana Lickety Split (page 226)

ASIAN

Year of the Dragon Wonton Soup (page 114)

Not-So-Fried Rice (page 154)

Kinpira (page 152)

Pad Thai (page 195)

Teriyaki Seaweed Salad (page 159)

Green Tea Ice Cream (page 232)

BREAKFAST IN BED

Wake Up Kiss (page 95)

Hazelnut Mocha Shake (page 53)

Sprouted Buckwheat Granola (page 65)

Oh! Sweet Nuthin' Pancakes (page 58)

Hungry-Man Avocado Cheese Scramble (page 57)

GREEK

Strawberry Sangria (page 89)

Red Pepper Hummus (page 130) with Rosemary Crackers (page 131)

Greek Salad with Cashew Feta (page 145)

Mediterranean Burgers (page 184)

Sweet Emotions Vanilla Pudding (page 251)

HEALING AND REJUVENATION

M&J Ultimate Shake (page 54)

Sweet Green Smoothie (page 66)

Original Green Juice (page 85)

Superfood Salad (page 156)

Save-the-World Super Veggie Tonic (page 86)

Electrolyte Lemonade (page 75)

Superfood Soup (page 110)

ITALIAN

Focaccia Bread (page 125)

Carrot and Red Pepper Bisque
(page 101)

Celery Caesar Salad (page 142)

Pesto Pizzas (page 193)

Chocolate Ganache Torte (page 231)

MEXICAN

Tepache (page 92)

Hazelnut Horchata (page 81)

Big Nachos (page 117)

Cactus Salad (page 139)

Red Enchiladas (page 196)

Mole Tacos (page 186)

PARTY HORS D'OEUVRES

Strawberry Sangria (page 89)

Cheese-Stuffed Jalapeños (page 121)

Taquitos with Paprika Sauce
(page 135)

Pesto Tomato Sliders (page 129)

Cucumber Summer Rolls (page 122)

Buddha-Bites Wontons (page 118)

Almond Butter Cups (page 224)

SEAFOOD

Warm Miso Soup (page 113)

Mock Salmon Pâté (page 127)

Sea Cakes with Cilantro Chutney
(page 132)

Creamy Wakame Seaweed Salad
(page 151)

Mint Chocolate Hearts (page 254)

SUMMER BBQ/PICNIC

Goji Lemonade (page 76)

Chlorophyll Lemonade (page 72)

Electrolyte Lemonade (page 75)

Sprouted Black Bean Chili (page 109)

Mock Chicken Sandwiches
(page 189)

Crystal Crunch Bars (page 236)

Black and White Cookies (page 227)

SUNDAY BRUNCH

Virgin Mimosa (page 93)

Sweet Black Magic Iced Coffee
(page 90)

Cinnamon Raisin Bagels (page 48)

Chia Porridge (page 47)

Tangy Coconut Yogurt (page 68)

Apple Bread (page 38)

Breakfast Burritos (page 44)

Montelimat Espresso Bonbons
(page 244)

SUSHI

Warm Miso Soup (page 113)

Atlantis Rolls (page 164)

Green Dragon Rolls (page 176)

Californication Rolls (page 169)

Tiger Rolls (page 205)

Green Tea Ice Cream (page 232)

On the Road Again (Again): Traveling and Eating Raw

Traveling can be challenging for even the least discerning eater. Raw foodists, often being among the most discerning, can be daunted by the idea of a trip away from the comforts of their own refrigerator. Travel, though, is so enjoyable and rewarding that it should be made as easy as possible when it comes to eating. A little preparation can go a long way towards ensuring that your meals are tasty, balanced, and satisfying, and not something you regret later! Even if you don't consume alcohol—it doesn't mean you won't wake up in Vegas with a food hangover!

The ideal trip, where healthful food is concerned, will have you staying in one place, with access to a refrigerator, in a town with great organic health food stores and raw restaurants, and surrounded by companions with similar food preferences. Traveling however, often involves family, business associates, adventure, and the unknown. Additionally, the best places on earth are often remote and uncivilized and with little infrastructure. In short, you may not have any of the aforementioned luxuries (or so they will seem once you're without them). Think carefully about the specifics of *your* trip and plan accordingly. It may or may not be your intention to eat raw foods exclusively while traveling. Either way, this advice may help.

Consider Packing These Foods

Nori Sheets—A sheet of nori can instantly turn any salad into a wrap.

Sea Salt—A small container of sea salt is great to use in restaurants or hotels when you don't want to add iodized table salt to your food. Small, travel sizes are available.

Munchies—Nuts, seeds, homemade or packaged raw snacks, crackers or trail mixes, raw protein bars, raw chocolate bars, and dried fruit are great on-the-road staples. Remember: goji berries are great for helping to protect against the effects of radiation exposure from flying.

Salad Improvers—Raw olives, whole-leaf dulse, and cold-pressed olive oil (packed in travel-size containers) can quickly convert a bag of organic greens into a delicious salad.

Green Powder—Pour green powder directly into a bottle of orange juice or water. This simple mixture can supply concentrated vitamins and minerals when you haven't been eating the most nutritious foods, supply extra energy while you're on the go, and even replace a meal in a pinch. Bring one powerful enough to combat jet lag or make up for a bad night's sleep on an inflatable bed. Pack the single-serving sizes or a full-size jar and a mini funnel.

Food from This Book—The following dishes travel well (we know from experience):

Apple Bread (page 38)

Cinnamon Raisin Bagels (page 48)

Blue Corn Chips (page 25)

RAWvolution's Famous Onion Bread (page 30)

Cheese-Stuffed Jalapeños (page 121)

Everyday Flax Crackers (page 126)

Rosemary Crackers (page 131)

Nuggy Buddies Mock Chicken Nuggets (page 218)

Crunchings and Munchings Squash Seeds (page 216)

Dinosaur Kale Chips (page 214)

Rootin' Tootin' Root Veggie Chips (page 222)

Tutti Frutti Fruit Chips (page 220)

Black and White Cookies (page 227)

Chocolate Chip Cookie Dough Balls (page 230)

Crystal Crunch Bars (page 236)

Ninja Protein Balls (page 247)

A CAUTIONARY TALE FOR THE RAW FOOD TRAVELER

One of the benefits of owning a raw food restaurant is that you can almost always get something good to eat. When we're about to head out of town, Janabai and I will often stop in at ELR on our way to the airport to pick up a snack or meal to go. One such night, we stopped in and poured ourselves two Durian Love Shakes—one for each of us. Soon after, we arrived at Los Angeles International Airport and began the familiar hustle of obtaining our boarding passes and shuffling our luggage from here to there. By the time we began to approach the security checkpoint, there was a small band of slightly panicked airport security personnel muttering inconspicuously about "a gas leak." Those familiar with durian will know that the fruit can be smelled from yards away and the fragrance is often likened to that of onions in the most flattering cases, or to dirty gym socks or gasoline in the least. By that time, we had finished our drinks so we discarded our empty cups and allowed the frenzied investigation to ensue behind us as we cooly made our way through security and towards our gate. I have no doubt that their searching eventually led them to the trash bin that held our cups and the remnants of our shakes. Who knew fruit could cause so much chaos!

Consider Packing These Supplies

Blender Bottle—This is a handy portable container for mixing liquids with powders while on the go.

Utensils—We like the reusable bamboo-style utensil sets, but extra corn-plastic takeout utensils from your favorite raw food restaurant can be reused too!

Knife and Cutting Board—A picnic-size set can be helpful on road trips and in hotels.

Napkins—These are always handy while eating on the go.

Consider This Regarding Water

Drinking quality water is very important but we don't love the idea of using mountains of plastic water bottles in the process or being exposed to the BPA in most plastics. If you are traveling by car, bring a refillable three-gallon BPA-free bottle (or a few gallon-sized bottles for easier pouring). You can refill these at health food stores and even some conventional grocery stores have reverse osmosis water filling machines. If you *are* buying water on the go, try to purchase the one-liter glass bottles.

Choose spring water when you can. There is no more natural source of living water than that from a natural cold spring! And, you get to experience the adventure of spring hunting! It will usually take you off the beaten tourist track. While traveling throughout

the country, we've experienced spring water so good, we considered moving nearby. Use FindaSpring.com to direct you to local springs wherever you are traveling and to advise you as to the quality of the water at each site. You may also wish to purchase a TDS meter, an inexpensive tool used to gauge the purity of the water for yourself. When you visit a spring, make sure to take with you as many empty bottles or jugs as you can carry!

Matt at Cricket Hill Spring, Black Mountain, North Carolina.

Other Tips

- Many large towns and cities have health food stores, food co-ops, and farmers' markets. Routing your drive past any of these to stock up can make healthful eating much easier and infinitely more satisfying than dining at restaurants you would normally not go to. We've been in Whole Foods Markets in nearly every state in which they exist as well as dozens of unique mom and pop places!

- Research raw, organic, and vegetarian restaurants before you leave for your trip—you may be surprised at how many there are throughout the country!

- Many restaurants will serve their veggie wraps in lettuce instead of bread. Ask them to hold the chicken and add avocado instead. Servers are usually very accommodating when asked politely.

- At Mexican restaurants, order the largest guacamole, the largest salsa, and a large plate of shredded lettuce with cilantro and make your own raw taco salad!

- Find a restaurant that offers a quality salad bar.

- Have us make it! Each week, RAWvolution creates a box of prepared, organic, raw foods that includes two savory soups, four gourmet entrees, four side dishes, and two delicious desserts. This provides packaged raw foods that you can bring with you on a flight, or have shipped to you overnight wherever in the fifty states you'll be! Pass on airplane "food" and order The Box at rawvolution.com.

- In a 2010 *Huffington Post* article, addressing air travel, Dr. Joseph Mercola stated, "If you fly at night you can reduce your radiation risk by 99 percent because nearly all of the radiation from the sun is being blocked by the earth."

- After a flight, be sure to reset your circadian clock by grounding your body to the earth. Go to the nearest park or outdoor space and sit at the foot of a tree or stand barefoot on the grass, close your eyes, and relax.

- Do your best to make the healthiest choices possible but also remember to relax and enjoy your trip!

What's Next? Our Hopes for the Future

Throughout this book, we have sprinkled bits of knowledge here and there from heroes of the raw food movement, which has been thriving since ancient times. Pythagoras, the eminent Greek philosopher, insisted his disciples become *apuratrophists* and eat their food *apura* or "unfired." The first raw food recipe book, *Uncooked Foods and How to Use Them* by Eugene Christian and Mollie Griswold Christian, was written in 1904, and the category has slowly but steadily been seen more prominently on bookstore shelves in recent years. More and more raw food restaurants are opening across the country, as are stores that cater to the living food lifestyle and sell raw products. All of this is great news. But what's next? Here are our hopes and dreams for the future.

Our Hopes for the Raw Foods Movement

THE NEW (BUT OLD) NORMAL

We hope to see raw foods achieve their rightful place in the cultural dialogue as "normal" food. It is only our recent obsession with convenience, price, and junk food that is truly "radical." The health food movement should not be a movement—healthful food should be the norm! If we shop at "health food stores" and eat "health food," what does everyone else call the foods they eat? That eating healthful food has become a movement only illuminates how poor a choice consuming the **S**tandard **A**merican **D**iet is. Clean food being viewed as some type of alternative makes it deceptively easy for agro-food conglomerates to control the debate as they can occupy the position of purveying "conventional" food. Why is non-organic food referred to as "conventional"? Shouldn't it be labeled "non-organic" so you'll know it contains pesticides, fungicides, herbicides, and insecticides? And why are we patrons of organic foods still paying more for the chemicals we're not using? Organic food should be less expensive than conventional, and if someone wants to pay more to subsidize the use of chemicals on their food, they can. We must reframe the conversation and the labels. Fruits and vegetables are normal foods. Cotton candy is not! Even if it's the "organic" cotton candy sold at some health food chains.

A LITTLE GOES A LONG WAY—A LOT GOES EVEN FURTHER

We hope you'll join us. We don't expect that cooking will go away. Even if it could, that's not necessarily what we want. We do hope that everyone becomes a raw foodist. Meaning, we hope everyone can recognize the value in raw foods and make an effort to integrate them into their lives to *some* degree. We don't want tapas bars or Grandma's soup to disappear, but we'd love for everyone to make informed choices and utilize the power of raw foods to improve their lives and health.

A SMALL CHANGE, BUT COMPLETELY DOABLE

We hope to see packaged raw food companies adopt a holistic approach to providing their goods for sale in the marketplace. For us, it's not enough that the snack inside the bag is organic and sprouted if the bag itself has a thousand-year half-life! To believe that it's okay to contribute mind-boggling amounts of petroleum-based elements into the environment for a single-serving food product is not cool. As consumers, we demand only sustainable packaging sourced from companies that are truly making an effort to heal the planet. Sustainable options already exist! We also hope raw food purveyors will focus more on pesticide-free and organic ingredients. Many packaged raw food

RAWvolution, New York City.

companies use conventional ingredients in order to meet consumer demand for low prices. Using non-organic ingredients, however, contributes to so many of the health and environmental ills that the raw food movement aspires to heal that it becomes counter-productive. We encourage consumers to continue to be good label readers and demand more from conventional and raw food products alike.

RAW STANDARDS

We hope to see a combined effort by the raw food community and raw food industry to adopt raw food certification. We believe this to be vitally important for protecting the integrity of live foods. As raw food becomes an increasingly popular concept, many companies are jumping on the bandwagon with products that often contain 50 to 100 percent cooked ingredients! We were astonished to find a protein bar that purported to contain "all raw ingredients" and actually had *no* raw ingredients! Raw food consumers are super savvy, but they shouldn't be expected to know esoteric food industry secrets in order to be able to confidently purchase a packaged raw snack. Furthermore, these types of controversies are off-putting to those who are less committed to the lifestyle or are just starting out. The "is it really raw?" debate is tiresome and should be put to rest by independent accreditation. Otherwise, "raw" runs the risk of facing the same dilution and eventual dissolution that befell the word "natural."

Our Hopes for Our Planet

A VOICE FOR THE VOICELESS

We hope to see animal testing, exploitation, and abuse end immediately. It is a tragedy of epic proportions and bodes ill for the preservation of our humanity. Like all things that are put under the weight of a corporate bottom line, animals have been reduced to mere assembly pieces or, rather, disassembly pieces. Because of the need for cheaper food and larger profits, animal welfare has been more than forgotten, it has been willfully disregarded. Being complicit in the crime that is factory farming, whether directly or indirectly, as a blind-eyed consumer, is a disgrace that rips away our compassion and moral grounding.

> The greatness of a nation and its moral progress can be judged by the way its animals are treated. —Mahatma Gandhi

Better choices are becoming available daily, whether you choose to be a vegan, vegetarian, or someone who eats animal products consciously with fervent attention to the welfare of the animals. Not only food, but also many cosmetics and household products are labeled to identify them as not having been tested on animals. We hope that the outcry at animal testing gets loud enough that our culture will give animals the dignity they deserve and stop using them as cheap commodity.

LET MY PEOPLE'S FOOD GO!

We hope that people are given legal access to raw and unpasteurized foods. The recent food scares and consequent legal actions that have ensnared raw almonds, raw dairy, unpasteurized kombucha, and kimchi give us cause for alarm. Food borne illnesses are not inherent to unheated foods. Improper food safety practices and contamination are the real culprits. Destroying foods with heat, irradiation, or other chemical practices only ensures that occurrences of contamination up to that point are eradicated. Without strong food safety measures, pasteurized food is as likely to be contaminated as living foods. The public deserves access to safe food, but that access should not be at the expense of that food's nutritional value. Furthermore, outlawing foods in their natural state is a slippery slope and at odds with the very concept of liberty. No plant should be illegal! Do we want a world where fresh strawberries are contraband? It may sound alarmist but that is now the case with raw almonds. As of 2007, the FDA mandated that almonds grown in the U.S. *must* be steam pasteurized (read: cooked), exposed to radiation (a universal carcinogen), or treated with propylene oxide (a probable human carcinogen)!

TRUTH IN LABELING

We hope to see genetically modified foods labeled as such. GM foods are dangerous to individuals, the environment, and the global food supply. We believe consumers are waking up to the importance of this issue, but without labeling standards it's difficult for consumers to purchase responsibly. Large food conglomerates agree with us, which is why they refuse to label genetically modified foods as such and vehemently oppose any attempt to legislate labeling. Genetically modified foods also beggar farmers as they enslave them to continually purchase patented, non-reproductive seed technologies. The great news is that there is a groundswell of activism on this front and many people are becoming aware of this extremely important issue.

COLONY RECOVERY

We hope that the bee populations can recover from the devastation they have faced in recent years. Colony collapse disorder, which they are suffering from in ever-increasing numbers, has the potential to become a "food collapse disorder." Fortunately, we have been aware of this potential for more than 50 years, thanks to brilliant minds like Albert Einstein and Rudolf Steiner. Unfortunately, we didn't listen to these celebrated geniuses and have done absolutely nothing about it in all this time! The internet however, is educating people at lightning speed. According to a United Nations report, of the 100 crop species that supply the world with 90 percent of its food, bees are responsible for pollinating 70 percent. Opinions on cause differ wildly, but it is clear to us that commercial beekeeping, combined with pesticide usage and the increasing encroachment of humans and technologies on natural habitats play a role in the sad state of bee affairs today. By supporting conscious and organic beekeeping operations, we help ourselves, our food supply, the planet, and the bees themselves.

Our Hopes for Our Health

BRING MEDICINE OUT OF THE DARK AGES

We hope that medical schools begin to require a more intensive study of nutrition. We wish that doctors realized the fundamental role of nutrition in preventing disease. They should work actively with their patients to correct dietary imbalances from the very beginning, before declaring conditions incurable or requiring an ever-deepening medicalization based on treatment protocols that only focus on the management of symptoms while ignoring causes. We hope too, that alternative therapies that are legal and being used effectively in other countries will be made legal here in the United States.

Let food be thy medicine and medicine be thy food. —Hippocrates

P. S.: The cure is the removal of the cause!

We are the RAWvolutionaries

We hope that you realize that we are all valuable links in a long chain of health pioneers and health freedom activists. Our work and intentions are vitally important in carrying on what is a long tradition of natural health. Scores of influential leaders and thinkers in all corners of the globe and of every persuasion have long advocated natural healing through a variety of methods and have seen astonishing results. The social struggle of natural healing against disease and ignorance is as old as society itself. We owe it to our future generations to guard the knowledge we have been handed, to strive to refine it, to increase awareness of it, and access to it!

A cool revolution, not a hot violent one— that continues as a gradual process of civilization that for all its slowness is steady in its progress and sure in its ultimate success. —Robert Thurman

ACKNOWLEDGMENTS

Our most heartfelt thanks to the following friends for their help with this book:

Brendan and Winter Armm, Jordana Bermudez, Rynn Berry, Sasha Beuerlein-Steinberg, Jeffrey Botticelli, Sarah Branham, Moises Chimil, Gigi Clark, Patricia Cooper, Ava Couture, Joel Cruz, Judith Curr, Zat Elias, Rick Ellis, Taylor Estes, Abel Garcia, Andrea Gómez Romero, Anneliese Gómez, Megan Greene, Hinton Harrison, Anna Inthavong, Sukhdev and Akahdahmah Jackson, Collette Keating, Gordon Kennedy, Steven Lam, Hedda Leonardi, Liesl Maggiori, Terezo Mendez, Zen and Bunni Nishimura, Nicholas Owens, Tanya Perez, Lisa Riley, James Romero, Gina Sabatella, Katie Tomer, Gretchen Victor, Daniella Wexler, Sand Wrenn, and James Wvinner.

GLOSSARY

Açaí Powder A powder made from the açaí berry, the fruit of the açaí palm. Açaí is native to Central and South America and contains essential fatty acids and high levels of antioxidants.

Apple Cider Vinegar A vinegar made from aged apple cider. Apple cider vinegar is rich in enzymes and potassium and helps to improve digestion and assimilation. Organic, unfiltered, and raw or unpasteurized is best.

Arame A species of dried kelp best known for its use in Japanese cuisine. Arame is high in calcium, iodine, iron, magnesium, and vitamin A.

Bee Pollen Is a mass of flower pollen, harvested as food for humans, that has been packed by worker honeybees into granules with added nectar, enzymes, and other compounds that increase its nutritional value. The exact chemical composition of pollen gathered depends on which plants the worker bees are gathering the pollen from, and can vary from hour to hour, day to day, week to week, and colony to colony, even in the same apiary, with no two samples of bee pollen being identical.

Bok Choy An East Asian leaf vegetable related to the Western cabbage, with smooth, dark green leaf blades emanating from a cluster reminiscent of celery.

Buckwheat Groats The hulled grains of buckwheat. Despite the name, buckwheat is not related to wheat, as it is not a grain or cereal but, instead, a plant related to sorrel and rhubarb.

Burdock Root The taproot of young burdock plants that are eaten as a root vegetable. While generally out of favor in modern European cuisine, it remains popular in Asia. In Japan, it's called *gobō*.

Cacao Butter A pale-yellow, pure, edible vegetable fat extracted from the fermented seeds of the cacao fruit.

Cacao Nibs Small pieces of the fermented seeds of the cacao fruit. These seeds are what all chocolate is made from. Raw cacao contains the trace minerals manganese, zinc, and copper as well as iron, chromium, magnesium, and omega-6 fatty acids.

Cacao Powder A powder made from the fermented seeds of the cacao fruit.

Chia Seeds The seeds of a flowering plant in the mint family. The name chia is derived from the Aztec word *chian,* meaning "oily." Chia seeds typically contain 20 percent protein, 34 percent oil, and 25 percent dietary fiber. The oil from chia seeds is one of the richest sources of omega-3 fatty acids. Chia seeds also contain phosphorus, manganese, calcium, and potassium. The soaked seeds are gelatinous in texture, lending themselves to use in porridges and puddings.

Chlorophyll The green pigment in plants that harnesses the sun's energy in photosynthesis. The chlorophyll molecule is chemically similar to human blood, except that its central atom is magnesium while blood's central atom is iron.

Coconut Aminos A raw and soy-free seasoning sauce made from the sap of the coconut palm.

Coconut Butter A spread made from whole coconut flesh, not just the oil, as is the case with coconut oil.

Coconut Meat The soft flesh found within a young coconut.

Coconut Nectar A low-glycemic sweetener made from the sap of the coconut palm.

Coconut Oil The oil pressed from the flesh of coconuts. Coconut oil contains up to 50 percent medium-chain saturated fatty acids, which have powerful anti-bacterial, anti-microbial, and anti-fungal properties. Coconut oil also has cholesterol-lowering properties, is an instant energy source, contains no cholesterol and no trans-fatty acid, and is not hydrogenated.

Coconut Sugar A sweetener produced from the sap of the flower buds of coconuts that has been used as a traditional sweetener for thousands of years in South East Asia. Coconut sugar is classified as a low glycemic index food and has a high mineral content, being a rich source of potassium, magnesium, zinc, and iron. In addition to this it contains vitamins B_1, B_2, B_3, and B_6.

Coconut Water The water found within the young Thai coconut. Coconut water contains essential electrolytes and a high potassium content and is very hydrating. There have been cases where coconut water has been used as an intravenous hydration fluid when medical saline was unavailable.

Collard Greens A leafy green vegetable from the same family as cabbage and broccoli. The large, flat leaves are perfect for using in place of tortillas for wraps.

Dr. Schulze's SuperFood Plus Powder An herbal supplement containing spirulina, blue-green algae, chlorella, barley, alfalfa, wheatgrass, dulse, beet root, spinach leaf, acerola cherry, rose hips, orange peel, lemon peel, and palm fruit in a base of saccharomyces cerevisiae yeast.

Dried Mulberries A dried fruit containing 3 grams of protein per ounce as well as iron, calcium, vitamin C, and resveratrol, an antioxidant compound that combats free-radical damage.

Dulse A dried, reddish-purple seaweed that grows on the northern coasts of the Atlantic and Pacific oceans. Dulse is a great source of protein, iron, potassium, iodine, and manganese.

E3 Live A wild-harvested, blue-green algae supplement in frozen/liquid form that contains 64 vitamins, minerals, and amino acids.

Flax Oil A yellowish oil cold pressed from the dried ripe seeds of the flax plant that is favored for its high levels of alpha-linolenic acid (ALA), a particular form of omega-3 fatty acid.

Flaxseeds Tiny brown or yellow/golden seeds rich in omega-3 fatty acids, calcium, iron, magnesium, potassium, and vitamin E.

Food Dehydrator A low-temperature "oven" used to gently dry fruit or prepared raw dishes creating drier, heartier, or crunchier textures while maintaining a food's nutritional integrity.

Food Processor An appliance used to assist in the chopping and shredding of vegetables and fruits and the grinding of nuts and seeds.

Goji Berries A dried fruit, slightly smaller than a raisin, and perhaps the most nutritionally rich fruit on the planet. Goji berries contain 18 kinds of amino acid, including all 8 essential amino acids, and up to 21 trace minerals. They are a very rich source of carotenoids, including beta-carotene, and contain vitamins C, B_1 (thiamine), B_2 (riboflavin), B_6 (pyridoxine), and E. Goji berries are regarded in Eastern medicine as a longevity food of the highest order.

Goldenberries Tart, dried berries, also known as "Incan Berries" and "Cape Gooseberries." They are an excellent source of vitamin A, vitamin C, carotene, and bioflavonoids.

Green Powder Essentially the raw food multi-vitamin, designed to be taken on a daily basis and especially during periods of cleansing or fasting. The best varieties contain a combination of raw, organic, and/or wild-crafted greens and cereal grasses, algaes, sea vegetables, superfoods, digestive enzymes, and probiotics. Billy's Infinity Greens, Pure Synergy, and Vitamineral Green are some of the very best.

Hemp Protein Powder A powdered concentration of the most proteinaceous part of the hemp seed containing up to 50 percent protein. Hemp protein also contains high amounts of zinc, iron, and magnesium, and an ideal balance of omega-3 and omega-6 fatty acids.

Hemp Seeds Tiny seeds with a nutty flavor containing over 30 percent digestible protein and rich in iron and vitamin E as well as omega-3 and omega-6 essential fatty acids.

High-Speed Blender A commercial-style blender with a two-horsepower (or larger) motor and a large pitcher. We recommend Vitamix.

Horseradish Root A spicy root from the mustard family that contains potassium, calcium, magnesium, and phosphorus.

Irish Moss A species of red algae which grows abundantly along the rocky parts of the Atlantic coast of Europe and North America. It is rich in iodine and sulfur and is commonly used as a natural thickening agent.

Juicer A machine that mechanically separates juice from the solid part (pulp) of most fruits, herbs, leafy greens, and vegetables. There are three main types of juicer: the centrifugal juicer that uses blades and a sieve to separate the juice from the pulp, the masticating juicer that "chews" fruit to a pulp before squeezing out the juice, and the triturating juicer that has twin gears that crush and press foods to separate the juice.

Jungle Peanuts Heirloom peanuts that are wild-harvested by hand in the jungles of the Amazon. Likely the original ancestors of all commercial peanuts grown today, they contain all 8 essential amino acids, vitamin E, and are free from aflatoxins, toxic chemical products produced by fungi that readily colonize commercial peanut crops.

Kelp Noodles Long, thin noodles made by stripping the outer skin from kelp exposing a clear interior. Kelp noodles have nearly no flavor of their own and tend to take on the flavor of whatever they're dressed with.

Kombucha An effervescent tea-based beverage that is often consumed for its anecdotal health benefits. Kombucha is available commercially and can be made at home by fermenting tea using a solid mass of yeast and bacteria that forms the kombucha culture, often referred to as the "mother." Normally, kombucha contains less than 0.5 percent alcohol, which classifies it as a nonalcoholic beverage.

Lucuma Powder A powder made from a subtropical fruit native to Peru's Andean region. This slightly maple-flavored fruit has long been a culinary favorite in Peru, where lucuma-flavored ice cream is more popular than chocolate ice cream! Lucuma is a great source of beta-carotene, niacin, vitamin B_3 (nicotinamide), and iron.

Maca Root Powder A powder made from a root vegetable native to the high Andes of Peru and Bolivia. Maca's history as a powerful strength and stamina enhancer and libido/fertility herb stretches back well over 500 years. Maca is a powerful adaptogen, which means it has the ability to balance and stabilize the body's

systems. Maca can help raise low blood pressure as well as lower high blood pressure. Maca is also high in iron and iodine.

Mandolin Slicer A device that slices vegetables and fruits to a desired thickness safely and quickly with a controlled back-and-forth motion over a V-shaped stainless steel blade.

Matcha A high-quality, stone-ground, Japanese green tea in the form of a fine powder. Matcha is made from shade-grown tea leaves and contains an exceptionally high amount of antioxidants.

Mesquite Powder A traditional Native American food made from ripened seedpods of the mesquite tree ground into a fine powder. Used as a staple food for centuries by desert dwellers, this high protein meal is also high in calcium, magnesium, potassium, iron, and zinc, and is rich in the amino acid lysine. It has a sweet, molasses-like flavor with a hint of caramel.

Miso A traditional Japanese seasoning paste produced by fermenting rice, barley, and soy or other beans with salt and a strain of fungi known as *kōji-kin*.

Nopalitos One of two foods derived from the prickly pear cactus (the other is the prickly pear or cactus fruit). *Nopal* means "cactus" in Spanish and *nopalitos* refers to the pads once they are cut up and prepared for eating.

Nori Square sheets of dried seaweed, typically used in sushi making. Raw nori sheets are black while the toasted sheets are green.

Nut Milk Bag A bag of fine mesh, often with a drawstring, used for straining juices and nut milks.

Nutritional Yeast A deactivated yeast in the form of flakes or powder. Nutritional yeast is considered a complete protein and contains B-complex vitamins. It has a somewhat cheesy flavor.

Peppermint Essential Oil A concentrated liquid of aroma compounds distilled from the peppermint plant.

Pomegranate Powder Freeze-dried pomegranate juice that has been milled into a fine powder that contains high levels of antioxidants.

Probiotics A supplement containing various strains of live microorganisms like those found in fermented foods such as sauerkraut, meant to improve the intestinal microbial balance.

Purple Corn Powder A raw flour made from dried Peruvian purple corn kernels that contain very high levels of antioxidants.

Reishi Mushroom Powder A powder made from a dried medicinal mushroom. Reishi has been used as a medicinal mushroom in traditional Chinese medicine for more than 2,000 years. Because of its astounding health benefits and absence of side effects, it has attained a reputation in the East as the ultimate herbal substance. Reishi has been found to lower blood cholesterol and blood sugar and is suspected to do far, far more. In China and Japan, reishi has been known by the following names: "sage mushroom," "auspicious mushroom," "divine mushroom," "herb of spiritual potency," and "mushroom of immortality."

Sea Lettuce An edible green algae that grows widely along the coasts of the world's oceans. It is high in protein and a variety of vitamins and minerals, especially iron.

Spirooli Slicer A three-in-one turning slicer that slices, shreds, and chips raw vegetables with stainless steel blade inserts.

Spirulina A fine powder dried from blue-green algae, offering 60 percent vegetable protein, vitamins B_1, B_2, B_3, B_6, B_9, C, D, A, and E. It is also a source of potassium, calcium, chromium, copper, iron, magnesium, manganese, phosphorus, selenium, sodium, and zinc.

Stevia A species of herb used as a sweetener and sugar substitute. As stevia extracts can register sweetness up to 300 times that of sugar, it has garnered attention with the rise in demand for low-carbohydrate, low-sugar food alternatives. Stevia also has a negligible effect on blood glucose levels. Stevia's taste has a slower onset and longer duration than that of sugar, although some of its extracts may have a bitter aftertaste at high concentrations.

Stone-Ground Mustard A more natural type of prepared mustard made from mustard seeds, apple cider vinegar, and sea salt.

Tahini A paste of ground sesame seeds used in North African, Greek, Turkish, and Middle Eastern cuisines. Tahini is an excellent source of copper, manganese, and the amino acid methionine, as well as a good source of vitamin B, zinc, iron, magnesium, and calcium.

Teeccino Herbal Coffee A caffeine-free blend of herbs, grains, fruits, and nuts with a flavor reminiscent of coffee.

Teflex Sheet A solid, nonstick, reusable sheet made of Teflon to be used when drying very moist or liquidy items in a food dehydrator.

Tocotrienols Vitamin E–rich compounds separated from rice bran and used as a powdered superfood supplement.

Ume Vinegar While not a true vinegar, this salty, sour liquid is a treasured byproduct of the pickling of umeboshi plums with salt and shiso, traditional in Japan.

Vanilla Bean Powder The minuscule seeds of the vanilla bean which is the hand-pollinated fruit pod of the vanilla orchid (the only fruiting orchid). This is vanilla in its most natural and delectable form.

Wakame A mild flavored sea vegetable or edible seaweed. Sea farmers have grown wakame for hundreds of years in Korea and Japan. Studies have found that a compound in wakame known as fucoxanthin can help burn fatty tissue.

Yacon Syrup Syrup made from an Andean plant that is a relative of the sunflower and used as a sweetener. Because of yacon's unique carbohydrate composition, it has little effect on blood sugar levels. Yacon is also a prebiotic, which feed probiotics in the gut, helping to maintain intestinal microbial balance. Yacon has a flavor reminiscent of caramel, molasses, and maple syrup.

Yerba Mate A hot, tea-like beverage made from a species of holly, native to subtropical South America. Mate contains potassium, magnesium, and manganese.

INDEX

A

Abramowski, O. L. M., 57
açai powder, 268
activism, 146
Agramonte, Krisztina, 43
ahbez, eden, 18, 98, 106
ahimsa diet, 15
alcoholic beverages, 8
Alexander, Joe, 162
almond butter:
    Almond Butter and Jelly
        Sandwiches, 210
    Almond Butter Cups, 224
    Almond Butter Shake, 34
    Ninja Protein Balls, 247
    Pad Thai, 195
Almond Milk, 24
    Chocolate Ganache Torte, 231
    see also nut milk
almond pulp, 24
    Black and White Cookies, 227
    Cinnamon Love French Toast,
        51
    Cinnamon Raisin Bagels, 48
    Deep Dish Spinach Pizza, 173
    Focaccia Bread, 125
    Rosemary Crackers, 131
almonds:
    Almond Butter Cups, 224
    Sweet Illusions Almond Bars,
        252
alternative medicine, 146, 266
Amsden, Janabai, 3–6, 11–12,
    259
Amsden, Matt, 2, 3–6, 9–11,
    259, 260
Anderson, Hans, 103
animal foods, 8
animal welfare, 264
appetizers, 115–36
    Big Nachos, 117
    Buddha-Bites Wontons, 118
    Cheese-Stuffed Jalapeños,
        121
    Cucumber Summer Rolls, 122
    Everyday Flax Crackers, 126
    Focaccia Bread, 125

    Mock Salmon Pâté, 127
    Pesto Bruschetta, 129
    Pesto Tomato Sliders, 129
    Red Pepper Hummus, 130
    Rosemary Crackers, 131
    Sea Cakes with Cilantro
        Chutney, 132
    Spinach Cheese Dip, 136
    Taquitos with Paprika Sauce,
        135
apple cider vinegar, 268
apples:
    Apple Bread, 38
        Almond Butter and Jelly
            Sandwiches, 210
    Tutti Frutti Fruit Chips, 220
appliances, 22
    food dehydrator, 7, 269
    food processor, 269
    juicer, 270
    mandolin slicer, 270
    Spirooli slicer, 271
arame, 268
    Holy Macro Bowl, 181
Arlin, Stephen, 197
Armstrong, Lawrence, 89
Asparagus Soup, Cream of, 104
astrology, 147
Avery, Phyllis, 182
avocados:
    Breakfast Burritos, 44
    Café Salad, 140
    Californication Rolls, 169
    Green Dragon Rolls, 176
    Guacamole, 28
    Hungry-Man Avocado Cheese
        Scramble, 57
    Red Enchiladas, 196–97
    Spinach Cheese Dip, 136
    Superfood Salad, 156
    Tiger Rolls, 205

B

bagels:
    Bagel Sandwiches, 167
    Cinnamon Raisin Bagels, 48

Baker, Art, 190
Baker, Elizabeth, 143
bananas:
    Almond Butter and Jelly
        Sandwiches, 210
    Banana Lickety Split, 226
    Banana Yogurt Chi Shake, 40
    Breakfast Bread, 43
    Nana-choco-squiter, 217
basil, *see* Pesto
Bazler, Thor, 197
bees, 265–66
    bee pollen, 268
beverages, *see* drinks
Bircher-Benner, Maximilian, 43
blender, high-speed, 269
bok choy, 268
    Indonesian Noodle Affair, 182
    Szechuan Noodles, 202
    Teriyaki Seaweed Salad, 159
Boots, Gypsy, 5, 98, 104, 109
Bragg, Patricia, 139
Bragg, Paul C., 84, 139
Brandt, Johanna, 75
Braunstein, Mark Mathew, 145
bread:
    Apple Bread, 38
        Almond Butter and Jelly
            Sandwiches, 210
    Breakfast Bread, 43
    Everyday Flax Crackers, 126
    Focaccia Bread, 125
    RAWvolution's Famous Onion
        Bread, 30
    Cocophoria Sandwiches,
        170
    Mediterranean Burgers,
        184
    Mock Chicken Sandwiches,
        189
    Mock Turkey Sandwiches,
        190
    Mushroom Swiss Burgers,
        192
    Pesto Pizzas, 193
    Reuben Sandwiches, 198
    Santorini Sandwiches, 208

Spicy Chipotle Burgers, 200–201
Vegetable Casserole, 206–7
Rosemary Crackers, 131
Vegetable Casserole, 206–7
breakfasts, 33–68
Almond Butter Shake, 34
Apple Bread, 38
Aztec Maca Shake, 36
Banana Yogurt Chi Shake, 40
Breakfast Bread, 43
Breakfast Burritos, 44
Chai Shake, 35
Chia Porridge, 47
Chocolate Durian Shake, 53
Cinnamon Love French Toast, 51
Cinnamon Raisin Bagels, 48
Durian Love Shake, 52
Hazelnut Mocha Shake, 53
Hungry-Man Avocado Cheese Scramble, 57
M&J Ultimate Shake, 54
Mango Smoothie, 61
Oh! Sweet Nuthin' Pancakes, 58
Spirulina Warrior Shake, 62
Sprouted Buckwheat Granola, 65
Strawberry Smoothie, 61
Sweet Green Smoothie, 66
Tangy Coconut Yogurt, 68
Über Protein Shake, 63
broccoli:
Cheesy Broccoli, 213
Szechuan Noodles, 202
Vegetable Casserole, 206–7
Yogi's Curried Vegetables, 160
Brook, Sapoty, 208
buckwheat, 268
Chocolate Buckwheat Tortugas, 228
Crystal Crunch Bars, 236
Dark Chocolate Peanut Butter Bars, 238
Sprouted Buckwheat Granola, 65
burdock root, 268
Kinpira, 152

Not-So-Fried Rice, 154
burgers:
Burger Patties, 26
Mediterranean Burgers, 184
Mushroom Swiss Burgers, 192
Spicy Chipotle Burgers, 200–201
Burritos, Breakfast, 44
Bushnoff, Fred, 98

C

cacao butter, 268
cacao nibs, 268
cacao powder, 268
Cactus Salad, 139
Calabrese, Karyn, 202
Carque, Otto, 71
Carrington, Hereward, 54
carrots:
Carrot and Red Pepper Bisque, 101
Cream of Carrot Soup, 104
Falafel Wraps, 174
Holy Macro Bowl, 181
Kinpira, 152
Mock Salmon Pâté, 127
Rootin' Tootin' Root Veggie Chips, 222
Save-the-World Super Veggie Tonic, 86
Sea Cakes with Cilantro Chutney, 132
Vegetable Casserole, 206–7
Witches' Brew, 96
cashews:
Cheesy Broccoli, 213
Cheesy Kale Chips, 214
Chocolate Ganache Torte, 231
Chocolate Ice Cream, 232
Cream Cheese, 26
Creamed Spinach, 143
Deep Dish Spinach Pizza, 173
Faux Egg, 27
Greek Salad with Cashew Feta, 145
Mediterranean Burgers, 184
Green Tea Ice Cream, 232
Indonesian Noodle Affair, 182
Mayo, 29

Montelimat Espresso Bonbons, 244
Nofu, 29
Oh! Sweet Nuthin' Pancakes, 58
Red Enchiladas, 196–97
Tiger Rolls, 205
Vanilla Ice Cream, 235
Vegetable Casserole, 206–7
Casserole, Vegetable, 206–7
cauliflower:
Californication Rolls, 169
Carrot and Red Pepper Bisque, 101
Vegetable Casserole, 206–7
Yogi's Curried Vegetables, 160
Cayce, Edgar, 148
celery:
Atlantis Rolls, 164
Burger Patties, 26
Celery Caesar Salad, 142
Mock Chicken Sandwiches, 189
Nuggy Buddies Mock Chicken Nuggets, 218
Original Green Juice, 85
Reuben Sandwiches, 198
Vegetable Casserole, 206–7
chai:
Chai Latte, 71
Chai Shake, 35
Chai Spider Ice Cream Float, 240
Chan, Mun, 252
cheese:
Cheesy Broccoli, 213
Cheesy Kale Chips, 214
Cream Cheese, 26
Bagel Sandwiches, 167
Cucumber Summer Rolls, 122
Santorini Sandwiches, 208
Greek Salad with Cashew Feta, 145
Hungry-Man Avocado Cheese Scramble, 57
Seed Cheese, 31
Cheese-Stuffed Jalapeños, 121
Mushroom Swiss Burgers, 192
Spinach Cheese Dip, 136

INDEX

chia seeds, 47, 268
  Chia Porridge, 47
chicken, mock:
  Mock Chicken Sandwiches, 189
  Nuggy Buddies Mock Chicken Nuggets, 218
children's favorites, 209–22
  Almond Butter and Jelly Sandwiches, 210
  Cheesy Broccoli, 213
  Cheesy Kale Chips, 214
  Crunchings and Munchings Squash Seeds, 216
  Dinosaur Kale Chips, 214
  Nana-choco-squiter, 217
  Nuggy Buddies Mock Chicken Nuggets, 218
  Rootin' Tootin' Root Veggie Chips, 222
  Tutti Frutti Fruit Chips, 220
Chili, Sprouted Black Bean, 109
chlorophyll, 268
  Chlorophyll Lemonade, 72
chocolate:
  Basic Chocolate, 25
  Almond Butter Cups, 224
  Banana Lickety Split, 226
  Black and White Cookies, 227
  Chocolate Buckwheat Tortugas, 228
  Dark Chocolate Peanut Butter Bars, 238
  Mint Chocolate Hearts, 254
  Montelimat Espresso Bonbons, 244
  Peppermint Patties, 248
  Sweet Illusions Almond Bars, 252
  Chocolate Chip Cookie Dough Balls, 230
  Chocolate Durian Shake, 53
  Chocolate Ganache Torte, 231
  Chocolate Ice Cream, 232
  Hazelnut Mocha Shake, 53
  Decadent Velvet Hot Chocolate, 241
  Fluffy Pudding Parfaits, 243
  Hot Chocolate, 82

Mole Tacos, 186
Motown Miracle, 83
Nana-choco-squiter, 217
Ninja Protein Balls, 247
Sugar-Free Chocolate Mousse, 251
Christian, Eugene, 47, 262
Christian, Mollie Griswold, 47, 262
cilantro:
  Creamy Wakame Seaweed Salad, 151
  Everyday Flax Crackers, 126
  Green Enchiladas, 178–79
  Guacamole, 28
  Salsa, 31
  Save-the-World Super Veggie Tonic, 86
  Sea Cakes with Cilantro Chutney, 132
cinnamon:
  Cinnamon Love French Toast, 51
  Cinnamon Raisin Bagels, 48
  Durian Love Shake, 52
  Hazelnut Horchata, 81
  Oh! Sweet Nuthin' Pancakes, 58
  Sprouted Buckwheat Granola, 65
  Tepache, 92
  Tutti Frutti Fruit Chips, 220
cleansing, 147
Clement, Brian, 167
coconut, shredded:
  Black and White Cookies, 227
  Peppermint Patties, 248
  Sweet Illusions Almond Bars, 252
coconut aminos, 268
coconut butter, 268
  Chocolate Chip Cookie Dough Balls, 230
coconut meat, 268
  Aztec Maca Shake, 36
  Breakfast Burritos, 44
  Carrot and Red Pepper Bisque, 101
  Chocolate Ice Cream, 232
  Cocophoria Sandwiches, 170
  Cool Cherry Cream Parfaits, 235

Fruit Tree Peach Cream Parfaits, 235
Green Enchiladas, 178–79
Green Tea Ice Cream, 232
Mango Smoothie, 61
Mock Turkey Sandwiches, 190
No-Egg Nog, 84
Peppermint Patties, 248
Red Enchiladas, 196–97
Strawberry Smoothie, 61
Sugar-Free Chocolate Mousse, 251
Sweet Emotions Vanilla Pudding, 251
Tangy Coconut Yogurt, 68
  Banana Yogurt Chi Shake, 40
Vanilla Ice Cream, 235
Yellow Wraps, 32
coconut nectar, 268
Basic Chocolate, 25
Chlorophyll Lemonade, 72
Chocolate Chip Cookie Dough Balls, 230
Chocolate Ganache Torte, 231
Cinnamon Nectar, 51
Fluffy Pudding Parfaits, 243
Green Tea Ice Cream, 232
Tepache, 92
Vanilla Ice Cream, 235
coconut oil, 268
  Montelimat Espresso Bonbons, 244
coconut sugar, 268–69
  Breakfast Bread, 43
coconut water, 269
  Almond Milk, 24
  Aztec Maca Shake, 36
  Chocolate Ice Cream, 232
  Gazpacho, 103
  Green Tea Ice Cream, 232
  Hazelnut Horchata, 81
  M&J Ultimate Shake, 54
  Mayo, 29
  Motown Miracle, 83
  Nana-choco-squiter, 217
  No-Egg Nog, 84
  Oh! Sweet Nuthin' Pancakes, 58
  Spirulina Warrior Shake, 62
  Superfood Soup, 110
  Vanilla Ice Cream, 235

Year of the Dragon Wonton
Soup, 114
coffee, *see* Teeccino herbal
coffee
collard greens, 269
Falafel Wraps, 174
compassion, 15
consciousness, 14–15
Cookies, Black and White, 227
Corn Chips, Blue, 25
Big Nachos, 117
corn powder, purple, 270
Cousens, Gabriel, 4, 5, 9, 174
crackers:
Everyday Flax Crackers, 126
Rosemary Crackers, 131
Pesto Bruschetta, 129
Vegetable Casserole, 206–7
cucumbers:
Cucumber Summer Rolls, 122
Original Green Juice, 85
Red Hot Chili Soup, 106
Santorini Sandwiches, 208
Save-the-World Super Veggie
Tonic, 86
Superfood Soup, 110
Curried Vegetables, Yogi's, 160

D

Dagger, Bob, 186
DeAndrea, Richard, 243
dehydrated foods, 7, 8
desserts and sweets, 223–54
Almond Butter Cups, 224
Banana Lickety Split, 226
Black and White Cookies, 227
Chai Spider Ice Cream Float,
240
Chocolate Buckwheat
Tortugas, 228
Chocolate Chip Cookie Dough
Balls, 230
Chocolate Ganache Torte, 231
Chocolate Ice Cream, 232
Cool Cherry Cream Parfaits,
235
Crystal Crunch Bars, 236
Dark Chocolate Peanut Butter
Bars, 238
Decadent Velvet Hot Chocolate,
241

Fluffy Pudding Parfaits, 243
Fruit Tree Peach Cream
Parfaits, 235
Green Tea Ice Cream, 232
Mint Chocolate Hearts, 254
Montelimat Espresso
Bonbons, 244
Ninja Protein Balls, 247
Peppermint Patties, 248
Sugar-Free Chocolate Mousse,
251
Sweet Emotions Vanilla
Pudding, 251
Sweet Illusions Almond Bars,
252
Vanilla Ice Cream, 235
Diamond, Harvey, 152
Diamond, Marilyn, 152
Diefenbach, Karl Wilhelm, 48
diversity of foods, 13
Dressing, Garlic Cream, 27
Drews, George Julius, 2, 7, 9, 13,
17, 58, 223, 256
Dr. Schulze's Superfood Plus
Powder, 269
drinks, 69–96
alcoholic, 8
Chai Latte, 71
Chai Spider Ice Cream Float,
240
Chlorophyll Lemonade, 72
Decadent Velvet Hot
Chocolate, 241
Electrolyte Lemonade, 75
Goji Lemonade, 76
Green Tea Latte, 79
Hawaiian Heat, 80
Hazelnut Horchata, 81
Herbal Iced Coffee
Concentrate, 28
Hot Chocolate, 82
Motown Miracle, 83
No-Egg Nog, 84
Original Green Juice, 85
Save-the-World Super Veggie
Tonic, 86
Strawberry Sangria, 89
Sweet Black Magic Iced
Coffee, 90
Tepache, 92
Virgin Mimosas, 93
Wake Up Kiss, 95

Witches' Brew, 96
see also shakes; smoothies
dulse, 269
durian, 259
Chocolate Durian Shake, 53
Durian Love Shake, 52

E

E3 Live, 269
earthing, 147
Edison, Thomas, 146
Egg, Faux, 27
Breakfast Burritos, 44
Hungry-Man Avocado Cheese
Scramble, 57
Ehret, Arnold, 62, 117, 126, 131
Eimer, Karl, 9, 189
Einstein, Albert, 266
Emerson, Ralph Waldo, 148
enchiladas:
Green Enchiladas, 178–79
Red Enchiladas, 196–97
enjoyment, 16
entrées, 163–208
Atlantis Rolls, 164
Bagel Sandwiches, 167
Californication Rolls, 169
Cocophoria Sandwiches, 170
Deep Dish Spinach Pizza, 173
Falafel Wraps, 174
Green Dragon Rolls, 176
Green Enchiladas, 178–79
Holy Macro Bowl, 181
Indonesian Noodle Affair, 182
Mediterranean Burgers, 184
Mexican Pizzas, 185
Mock Chicken Sandwiches, 189
Mock Turkey Sandwiches, 190
Mole Tacos, 186
Mushroom Swiss Burgers,
192
Pad Thai, 195
Pesto Pizzas, 193
Red Enchiladas, 196–97
Reuben Sandwiches, 198
Santorini Sandwiches, 208
Spicy Chipotle Burgers,
200–201
Szechuan Noodles, 202
Tiger Rolls, 205
Vegetable Casserole, 206–7

environmentalism, 148
Erasmus, Udo, 154
Essenes, 35, 80
Esser, William, 101
Estes, E. L. Moraine, 79
Estes, St. Louis, 76, 79
Euphoria Company, The, 5
Euphoria Loves RAWvolution, 6

F

Falafel Wraps, 174
family, 16
farms, 8
Fathman, Doris, 126
Fathman, George, 126
Faulkner, James, 72
Fidus, 48
flax oil, 269
flaxseeds, 269
    Apple Bread, 38
    Bagel Sandwiches, 167
    Blue Corn Chips, 25
    Breakfast Bread, 43
    Cheese-Stuffed Jalapeños,
        121
    Cinnamon Love French Toast,
        51
    Cinnamon Raisin Bagels, 48
    Deep Dish Spinach Pizza, 173
    Everyday Flax Crackers, 126
    Focaccia Bread, 125
    RAWvolution's Famous Onion
        Bread, 30
    Rosemary Crackers, 131
Fletcher, Horace, 52
food dehydrator, 7, 269
food processor, 269
food self-sufficiency, 148
Franklin, Benjamin, 147
freezing, 8
French Toast, Cinnamon Love, 51
friends, 16
Fry, T. C., 135, 182, 205
Fuhrman, Joel, 192
fundamental recipes, 24–32
    Almond Milk, 24
    Basic Chocolate, 25
    Blue Corn Chips, 25
    Burger Patties, 26
    Cream Cheese, 26
    Faux Egg, 27

Garlic Cream Dressing, 27
Guacamole, 28
Herbal Iced Coffee
    Concentrate, 28
Mayo, 29
Nofu, 29
Pesto, 30
RAWvolution's Famous Onion
    Bread, 30
Salsa, 31
Seed Cheese, 31
Taco Meat, 32
Yellow Wraps, 32
future, hopes for, 262–66

G

Gallo, Roe, 228
Gandhi, Mohandas K., 38, 40,
    81, 264
garlic:
    Garlic Cream Dressing, 27
    Mayo, 29
Gazpacho, 103
genetically modified foods, 265
Gerras, Charles, 151
Gerson, Max, 96
Gibran, Kahlil, 149
ginger:
    Goji Lemonade, 76
    Hawaiian Heat, 80
    Original Green Juice, 85
Glaser, Stan, 142
glossary, 268–71
goji berries, 258, 269
    Goji Lemonade, 76
goldenberries, 269
    Crystal Crunch Bars, 236
Goodman, Linda, 185
Graham, Douglas, 181
Graham, Sylvester, 36
Granola, Sprouted Buckwheat,
    65
Graser, Gusto, 48
green powder, 21, 29, 54, 247,
    259, 269
greens:
    Café Salad, 140
    Green Dragon Rolls, 176
    Superfood Salad, 156
    Sweet Green Smoothie, 66
    see also kale; lettuce; spinach

Gregory, Dick, 136
Griesse, Carolyn, 145
grounding, 147
Guacamole, 28
    Big Nachos, 117
    Mexican Pizzas, 185
    Mole Tacos, 186
    Taco Salad, 162
Guttzeit, Johannes, 48

H

Halfmoon, Hygeia, 240
Harrelson, Woody, 243
hazelnut:
    Hazelnut Horchata, 81
    Hazelnut Mocha Shake, 53
health, 13–14
hemp protein powder, 269
hemp seeds, 269
    Crystal Crunch Bars, 236
herbs, 20
Hesse, Herman, 48
Hippocrates, 266
Honiball, Essie, 131, 139
horseradish root, 269
Hotema, Hilton, 122
Hovannessian, Arshavir Ter, 125
Howell, Edward, 9, 93
Hoyt, Dan, 252
Hummus, Red Pepper, 130
    Falafel Wraps, 174
    Mediterranean Burgers, 184

I

ice cream:
    Chocolate Ice Cream, 232
        Chocolate Durian Shake,
            53
        Hazelnut Mocha Shake, 53
    Green Tea Ice Cream, 232
    Vanilla Ice Cream, 235
        Almond Butter Shake, 34
        Banana Lickety Split, 226
        Chai Shake, 35
        Chai Spider Ice Cream
            Float, 240
Irish Moss Gel, 29
    Faux Egg, 27
    Montelimat Espresso
        Bonbons, 244

Nofu, 29
Iyengar, B. K. S., 149

J

Jalapeños, Cheese-Stuffed, 121
Jean, Gypsy, 98
Jefferson, Thomas, 148
Jensen, Bernard, 110
Jubb, Annie Padden, 173
Jubb, David, 173
juicer, 270
Juliano, 193
Jung, Carl, 147
Just, Adolf, 38, 40

K

kale:
    Cheesy Kale Chips, 214
    Dinosaur Kale Chips, 214
    Holy Macro Bowl, 181
    Save-the-World Super Veggie
        Tonic, 86
    Simple Kale Salad, 155
    Superfood Salad, 156
Karas, Jim, 145
kelp noodles, 270
    Indonesian Noodle Affair, 182
    Pad Thai, 195
Kidson, Don, 4, 170
King, Martin Luther, Jr., 16
Kinpira, 152
Kirschner, H. E., 121
Klein, David, 205
Klein, Josua, 48
Kohler, John, 241
kombucha, 270
Koonin, Paul M., 90
Kordich, Jay, 164
Kouchakoff, Paul, 82
Krok, Morris, 131
Kuhne, Louis, 38, 131
Kulvinskas, Viktoras, 127, 130

L

LaTham, Aris, 140
latte:
    Chai Latte, 71
    Green Tea Latte, 79
lemons:

Chlorophyll Lemonade, 72
Electrolyte Lemonade, 75
Goji Lemonade, 76
Hawaiian Heat, 80
Strawberry Sangria, 89
lettuce:
    Breakfast Burritos, 44
    Celery Caesar Salad, 142
    Cocophoria Sandwiches, 170
    Green Enchiladas, 178–79
    Mediterranean Burgers, 184
    Mock Turkey Sandwiches, 190
    Mushroom Swiss Burgers, 192
    Red Enchiladas, 196–97
    Spicy Chipotle Burgers,
        200–201
    Taco Salad, 162
lifestyle, 146–49
Loux, Renée, 224
Lovewisdom, Johnny, 118, 131
lucuma powder, 270
Lust, Benedict, 61

M

maca root powder, 270
    Aztec Maca Shake, 36
Macfadden, Bernarr, 44
main dishes, *see* entrées
Malkmus, George, 2, 156
Malkmus, Rhonda, 156
mandolin slicer, 270
mango:
    Green Enchiladas, 178–79
    Mango Smoothie, 61
    Red Enchiladas, 196–97
Markowitz, Elysa, 232
matcha, 270
Mayo, 29
    Mock Chicken Sandwiches,
        189
    Nuggy Buddies Mock Chicken
        Nuggets, 218
McCabe, John, 190
McDermott, Stella, 65
Mead, Margaret, 146
medicine:
    alternative, 146, 266
    modern, 266
    traditional, 14
meditation, 148
menus, 256–57

Mercola, Joseph, 261
mesquite powder, 270
Meyerowitz, Steve, 159
miso, 113, 270
    Warm Miso Soup, 113
Mitchell, Teresa, 117
Mocha Shake, Hazelnut, 53
Mole Tacos, 186
Mousse, Sugar-Free Chocolate,
    251
mulberries, 269
    Breakfast Bread, 43
mushroom powder, purple,
    270–71
mushrooms:
    Burger Patties, 26
    Californication Rolls, 169
    Mushroom Swiss Burgers, 192
    Reuben Sandwiches, 198
    Spicy Chipotle Burgers,
        200–201
    Vegetable Casserole, 206–7
music, 18
mustard, stone-ground, 271

N

Nachos, Big, 117
Nagel, Gustav, 48
Napoleon I, Emperor, 149
Nature Boys, 98, 106, 109
Naturmenschen, 48, 51, 85
Nofu, 29
    Holy Macro Bowl, 181
Nolfi, Kristine, 113
nopalitos (nopales), 139, 270
    Cactus Salad, 139
noodles:
    kelp, 270
        Indonesian Noodle Affair,
            182
        Pad Thai, 195
    Szechuan Noodles, 202
nori, 258, 270
    Atlantis Rolls, 164
    Californication Rolls, 169
    Green Dragon Rolls, 176
    Indonesian Noodle Affair, 182
    Mexican Pizzas, 185
    Mole Tacos, 186
    Superfood Salad, 156
nut butters, 19

Nut Milk, 24
  Almond Butter Shake, 34
  Almond Milk, 24
    Chocolate Ganache Torte, 231
  Banana Yogurt Chi Shake, 40
  Chai Latte, 71
  Chai Shake, 35
  Chai Spider Ice Cream Float, 240
  Chia Porridge, 47
  Chocolate Durian Shake, 53
  Cream of Asparagus Soup, 104
  Cream of Carrot Soup, 104
  Durian Love Shake, 52
  Electrolyte Lemonade, 75
  Green Tea Latte, 79
  Hazelnut Mocha Shake, 53
  Hot Chocolate, 82
  M&J Ultimate Shake, 54
  Motown Miracle, 83
  Nana-choco-squiter, 217
  Sweet Black Magic Iced Coffee, 90
  Sweet Green Smoothie, 66
  Über Protein Shake, 63
nut milk bag, 270
nutritional yeast, 270
nuts, 19

O
Ober, Clint, 147
oils, 19
onions:
  Bagel Sandwiches, 167
  Cocophoria Sandwiches, 170
  Guacamole, 28
  Mediterranean Burgers, 184
  Mock Chicken Sandwiches, 189
  Mushroom Swiss Burgers, 192
  Not-So-Fried Rice, 154
  RAWvolution's Famous Onion Bread, 30
  Spicy Chipotle Burgers, 200–201
  Vegetable Casserole, 206–7
orange:
  Cucumber Summer Rolls, 122
  Virgin Mimosas, 93

organic food, 8, 263
outdoorism, 148

P
Pad Thai, 195
Pancakes, Oh! Sweet Nuthin', 58
parfaits:
  Cool Cherry Cream Parfaits, 235
  Fluffy Pudding Parfaits, 243
  Fruit Tree Peach Cream Parfaits, 235
parsley:
  Original Green Juice, 85
  Save-the-World Super Veggie Tonic, 86
  Vegetable Casserole, 206–7
  Witches' Brew, 96
parsnips:
  Rootin' Tootin' Root Veggie Chips, 222
  Vegetable Casserole, 206–7
pasteurized foods, 265
peanuts, jungle, 270
  Banana Lickety Split, 226
  Dark Chocolate Peanut Butter Bars, 238
Peach Cream Parfaits, Fruit Tree, 235
Pearl, Bill, 155
peppermint essential oil, 270
  Mint Chocolate Hearts, 254
  Peppermint Patties, 248
peppers:
  Carrot and Red Pepper Bisque, 101
  Cheese-Stuffed Jalapeños, 121
  Holy Macro Bowl, 181
  Indonesian Noodle Affair, 182
  Red Pepper Hummus, 130
    Falafel Wraps, 174
    Mediterranean Burgers, 184
Pester, Bill, 51
Pesto, 30
  Pesto Bruschetta, 129
  Pesto Pizzas, 193
  Pesto Tomato Sliders, 129
philosophy, 13–16
pineapple:

Hawaiian Heat, 80
  Tepache, 92
pizzas:
  Deep Dish Spinach Pizza, 173
  Mexican Pizzas, 185
  Pesto Pizzas, 193
pomegranate powder, 270
  Crystal Crunch Bars, 236
Porridge, Chia, 47
Pottenger, Francis M., Jr., 92
Pranayama, 149
probiotics, 271
protein, 63
  Ninja Protein Balls, 247
  Spirulina Warrior Shake, 62
  Über Protein Shake, 63
pudding:
  Fluffy Pudding Parfaits, 243
  Sweet Emotions Vanilla Pudding, 251
purple corn powder, 271
Pythagoras, 34, 262

R
raisins:
  Breakfast Bread, 43
  Cinnamon Raisin Bagels, 48
  Crystal Crunch Bars, 236
  Sprouted Buckwheat Granola, 65
raw foods:
  benefits of, 9–12
  defined, 7–8
  hopes for future of, 262–66
  stocking kitchen with, 19–22
RAWvolution, 6
Reid, Daniel, 160
reishi mushroom powder, 271–72
responsibility, 14
restaurants, 261
Richter, John, 66, 104, 106
Richter, Vera, 66, 104, 106
Rose, Buddy, 98
Rosemary Crackers, 131
  Pesto Bruschetta, 129
  Vegetable Casserole, 206–7

S
Safron, Jeremy, 224
salads, 137–62, 258

Cactus Salad, 139
Café Salad, 140
Celery Caesar Salad, 142
Creamy Wakame Seaweed
    Salad, 151
Greek Salad with Cashew
    Feta, 145
Holy Macro Bowl, 181
Kinpira, 152
Simple Kale Salad, 155
Superfood Salad, 156
Taco Salad, 162
Teriyaki Seaweed Salad, 159
Salmon Pâté, Mock, 127
Salomonson, Ralph, 48
Salsa, 31
    Mexican Pizzas, 185
salt, sea, 258
sandwiches:
    Bagel Sandwiches, 167
    Cocophoria Sandwiches, 170
    Mediterranean Burgers, 184
    Mock Chicken Sandwiches,
        189
    Mock Turkey Sandwiches, 190
    Mushroom Swiss Burgers, 192
    Reuben Sandwiches, 198
    Santorini Sandwiches, 208
    Spicy Chipotle Burgers,
        200–201
Santillo, Humbart, 184
Schwarzenegger, Arnold, 155
Scott, William D., 251
seasonal eating, 13–14
seaweed, 20
    arame, 268
        Holy Macro Bowl, 181
    Creamy Wakame Seaweed
        Salad, 151
    kelp noodles, 270
        Indonesian Noodle Affair,
            182
        Pad Thai, 195
    nori, 258, 270
        Atlantis Rolls, 164
        Californication Rolls, 169
        Green Dragon Rolls, 176
        Indonesian Noodle Affair,
            182
        Mexican Pizzas, 185
        Mole Tacos, 186
        Superfood Salad, 156

sea lettuce, 271
    Sea Cakes with Cilantro
        Chutney, 132
    Teriyaki Seaweed Salad,
        159
seed butters, 19
seeds, 19
Semple, Dugald, 114, 131
sesame seeds:
    Indonesian Noodle Affair, 182
    Kinpira, 152
    A Night in Tunisia Spicy
        Sesame Soup, 98
Sexauer, Hermann, 85
shakes:
    Almond Butter Shake, 34
    Aztec Maca Shake, 36
    Banana Yogurt Chi Shake, 40
    Chai Shake, 35
    Chocolate Durian Shake, 53
    Durian Love Shake, 52
    Hazelnut Mocha Shake, 53
    M&J Ultimate Shake, 54
    Spirulina Warrior Shake, 62
    Über Protein Shake, 63
    see also smoothies
Shannon, Nomi, 248
sharing food, 16
Shelton, Herbert, 83, 135
Sheridan, Jameth, 9, 169
Sheridan, Kim, 169
side dishes, 137–62
    Creamed Spinach, 143
    Kinpira, 152
    Not-So-Fried Rice, 154
    Yogi's Curried Vegetables, 160
Sikinger, Maximilian, 98, 104
slicers:
    mandolin, 270
    Spirooli, 271
smoothies, 33, 109
    Mango Smoothie, 61
    Strawberry Smoothie, 61
    Sweet Green Smoothie, 66
    see also shakes
Soria, Cherie, 244
soups, 97–114
    Carrot and Red Pepper
        Bisque, 101
    Cream of Asparagus Soup, 104
    Cream of Carrot Soup, 104
    Gazpacho, 103

A Night in Tunisia Spicy
    Sesame Soup, 98
Red Hot Chili Soup, 106
Sprouted Black Bean Chili, 109
Superfood Soup, 110
Warm Miso Soup, 113
Year of the Dragon Wonton
    Soup, 114
spices, 20
spinach:
    Creamed Spinach, 143
    Deep Dish Spinach Pizza, 173
    Greek Salad with Cashew
        Feta, 145
    Green Enchiladas, 178–79
    Save-the-World Super Veggie
        Tonic, 86
    Spinach Cheese Dip, 136
    Vegetable Casserole, 206–7
spirituality, 149
Spirooli slicer, 271
spirulina, 271
    Spirulina Warrior Shake, 62
    Sweet Green Smoothie, 66
Squash Seeds, Crunchings and
    Munchings, 216
Steiner, Rudolf, 266
stevia, 271
stone-ground mustard, 271
strawberries:
    Almond Butter and Jelly
        Sandwiches, 210
    Electrolyte Lemonade, 75
    Fluffy Pudding Parfaits, 243
    Strawberry Sangria, 89
    Strawberry Smoothie, 61
sunflower seeds:
    Apple Bread, 38
    Atlantis Rolls, 164
    Mock Chicken Sandwiches,
        189
    Nuggy Buddies Mock Chicken
        Nuggets, 218
    RAWvolution's Famous Onion
        Bread, 30
    Seed Cheese, 31
        Cheese-Stuffed Jalapeños,
            121
        Mushroom Swiss Burgers,
            192
        Spicy Chipotle Burgers,
            200–201

sungazing, 149
superfoods, 21
sweeteners, 21
Szekely, Edmond Bordeaux, 80

T

Taco Meat, 32
    Big Nachos, 117
    Green Enchiladas, 178–79
    Mexican Pizzas, 185
    Mole Tacos, 186
    Taco Salad, 162
    Taquitos with Paprika Sauce, 135
Tacos, Mole, 186
tahini, 271
    Pad Thai, 195
tea:
    Green Tea Ice Cream, 232
    Green Tea Latte, 79
    matcha, 270
Teeccino herbal coffee, 271
    Herbal Iced Coffee
        Concentrate, 28
        Hazelnut Mocha Shake, 53
        Sweet Black Magic Iced
            Coffee, 90
    Montelimat Espresso
        Bonbons, 244
    Wake Up Kiss, 95
Teflex sheet, 271
Thomas, Julian P., 53
Thoreau, Henry David, 148
Thurman, Robert, 266
Tobe, John H., 10, 132
tocotrienols, 271
    Sweet Green Smoothie, 66
tomatoes:
    Bagel Sandwiches, 167
    Cactus Salad, 139
    Café Salad, 140
    Cocophoria Sandwiches, 170
    Everyday Flax Crackers, 126
    Falafel Wraps, 174
    Gazpacho, 103
    Guacamole, 28
    Mock Chicken Sandwiches, 189
    Mock Turkey Sandwiches,190

Mole Tacos, 186
Nuggy Buddies Mock Chicken
    Nuggets, 218
Pesto Tomato Sliders, 129
Red Enchiladas, 196–97
Red Hot Chili Soup, 106
Rootin' Tootin' Root Veggie
    Chips, 222
Salsa, 31
Santorini Sandwiches, 208
Save-the-World Super Veggie
    Tonic, 86
Spicy Chipotle Burgers,
    200–201
Sprouted Black Bean Chili,
    109
Superfood Salad, 156
Vegetable Casserole, 206–7
tools, 22
Torte, Chocolate Ganache, 231
traveling, 258–61
Turkey Sandwiches, Mock, 190

U

ume vinegar, 271

V

vanilla bean powder, 271
Vanilla Ice Cream, 235
    Almond Butter Shake, 34
    Banana Lickety Split, 226
    Chai Shake, 35
    Chai Spider Ice Cream Float,
        240
Vetrano, Vivian Virginia, 176
Virtanen, Artturi, 95

W

wakame, 271
    Creamy Wakame Seaweed
        Salad, 151
Walker, Norman, 86
Wallace, Bob, 98
walnuts:
    Breakfast Bread, 43
    Burger Patties, 26
    Crystal Crunch Bars, 236

Dark Chocolate Peanut Butter
    Bars, 238
Mock Salmon Pâté, 127
Pesto, 30
Spinach Cheese Dip, 136
Sprouted Buckwheat Granola,
    65
Taco Meat, 32
water, 260
Wigmore, Ann, 127, 130
Wolfe, David, 2, 4, 195
Wontons, Buddha-Bites, 118
    Year of the Dragon Wonton
        Soup, 114
Wood, John, 243
Wraps, Falafel, 174
Wraps, Yellow, 32
    Buddha-Bites Wontons, 118
    Taquitos with Paprika Sauce,
        135
    Tiger Rolls, 205

Y

yacon syrup, 271
    Montelimat Espresso
        Bonbons, 244
yeast, nutritional, 270
yerba mate, 271
    Wake Up Kiss, 95
Yod, Father, 135
yoga, 149
Yogananda, Paramahansa, 149
Yogurt, Tangy Coconut, 68
    Banana Yogurt Chi Shake, 40

Z

Zimmerman, Emile, 98
zucchini:
    Cinnamon Love French Toast,
        51
    Cinnamon Raisin Bagels, 48
    Focaccia Bread, 125
    Red Hot Chili Soup, 106
    Red Pepper Hummus, 130
    Rootin' Tootin' Root Veggie
        Chips, 222
    Szechuan Noodles, 202
    Yogi's Curried Vegetables, 160